Cambridge Elements

Elements in Critical Heritage Studies
edited by
Kristian Kristiansen
University of Gothenburg
Michael Rowlands
UCL

WHY HISTORIC PLACES MATTER EMOTIONALLY

Responses – Attachments – Communities

Rebecca Madgin
University of Glasgow

Shaftesbury Road, Cambridge CB2 8EA, United Kingdom

One Liberty Plaza, 20th Floor, New York, NY 10006, USA

477 Williamstown Road, Port Melbourne, VIC 3207, Australia

314–321, 3rd Floor, Plot 3, Splendor Forum, Jasola District Centre, New Delhi – 110025, India

103 Penang Road, #05–06/07, Visioncrest Commercial, Singapore 238467

Cambridge University Press is part of Cambridge University Press & Assessment, a department of the University of Cambridge.

We share the University's mission to contribute to society through the pursuit of education, learning and research at the highest international levels of excellence.

www.cambridge.org
Information on this title: www.cambridge.org/9781009598521
DOI: 10.1017/9781009349413

© Rebecca Madgin 2025

This publication is in copyright. Subject to statutory exception and to the provisions of relevant collective licensing agreements, with the exception of the Creative Commons version the link for which is provided below, no reproduction of any part may take place without the written permission of Cambridge University Press & Assessment.

An online version of this work is published at doi.org/10.1017/9781009349413 under a Creative Commons Open Access license CC-BY-NC 4.0 which permits re-use, distribution and reproduction in any medium for non-commercial purposes providing appropriate credit to the original work is given and any changes made are indicated. To view a copy of this license visit https://creativecommons.org/licenses/by-nc/4.0

When citing this work, please include a reference to the DOI 10.1017/9781009349413

First published 2025

A catalogue record for this publication is available from the British Library

ISBN 978-1-009-59852-1 Hardback
ISBN 978-1-009-34943-7 Paperback
ISSN 2632-7074 (online)
ISSN 2632-7066 (print)

Additional resources for this publication at www.cambridge.org/historicplaces

Cambridge University Press & Assessment has no responsibility for the persistence or accuracy of URLs for external or third-party internet websites referred to in this publication and does not guarantee that any content on such websites is, or will remain, accurate or appropriate.

For EU product safety concerns, contact us at Calle de José Abascal, 56, 1°, 28003 Madrid, Spain, or email eugpsr@cambridge.org.

Why Historic Places Matter Emotionally

Responses – Attachments – Communities

Elements in Critical Heritage Studies

DOI: 10.1017/9781009349413
First published online: October 2025

Rebecca Madgin
University of Glasgow

Author for correspondence: Rebecca Madgin, rebecca.madgin@glasgow.ac.uk

Abstract: This Element explores why historic urban places matter emotionally. To achieve this, the Element develops a conceptual framework that breaks down the broad category of 'emotion' into three interrelated parts: (1) emotional responses, (2) emotional attachments, and (3) emotional communities. In so doing, new lines of enquiry are opened up, including the reasons why certain emotional responses such as pride and fear are provoked by historic urban places, the complex interplay of the physical environment and everyday experiences in informing emotional attachments, as well as the reasons why emotional communities coalesce in particular historic urban places. In addition, the Element explores the ways in which emotion, in the form of responses, attachments, and communities, can be considered within heritage management, and concludes with a discussion of where next for heritage theories and practices. This title is also available as Open Access on Cambridge Core.

This Element also has a video abstract: www.cambridge.org/madginabstract

Keywords: heritage, emotion, place, attachment, planning

© Rebecca Madgin 2025

ISBNs: 9781009598521 (HB), 9781009349437 (PB), 9781009349413 (OC)
ISSNs: 2632-7074 (online), 2632-7066 (print)

Contents

1 Introduction: Reconceptualising Emotion   1

2 Emotional Responses   15

3 Emotional Attachments   28

4 Emotional Communities   39

5 Recognising Emotion   52

6 Conclusion: A Future for Emotion   68

   References   75

1 Introduction: Reconceptualising Emotion

Saturday, 2 p.m., and I'm on the way to 'the match', a walk I've done hundreds of times. I cross the road and the steel girders at the top of the nineteenth-century stadium rise out of the tight-knit terraced housing that envelops this iconic structure that has shaped so many dreams, desires, hopes, and fears. With every footstep, my sense of anticipation and excitement rises. I enter the stadium and hit a wall of sound – a cacophony of chants, cheers, and jeers as the familiar songs reverberate around the stadium. I take my seat and my individual responses to the physical environment are immediately drawn into a collective sense of belonging – of 'my' and 'our' team as we join together to support the club. Over the course of the next two hours, my senses are alive, and I run through a range of emotional responses – anger, joy, fear, sadness, and pride each congeal into an emotional blur that both merges with and diverges from the emotions of others within the same stadium. The stadium and its surrounds fizz with emotional energy.

This walk, this stadium, and these experiences rush back to me as I read several stories of stadium closures as clubs seek to modernise through demolition and relocation. I think about this in the context of 'my' stadium and a wave of complex emotions run through me. I start to turn over the memories in my mind, I immerse myself in the collective folklore, I wonder about the other fans, I trace the words of the songs, I visualise the goals, the saves, and the near misses, and as I do so my mind and body unite in a sense of longing – to return, to replay, to revive. I'm now geographically distant but remain emotionally entangled. In this moment all my experiences merge and my profound emotional attachment to this 100-year-old stadium, with all its attendant memories and stories, becomes viscerally obvious to me.

This vignette captures why I wanted to explore why historic places matter emotionally. I know that we, individually and collectively, develop emotional relationships to certain places but I also know that it is difficult to explain why we feel this way, and even harder to recognise within heritage practice. This stadium is not listed, it is afforded no official historical or architectural value, but to the hundreds of thousands of people who enter through the turnstiles each year it has a value that sits outside of heritage designation. A sceptical reader could say that my experience is atypical yet there is a significant body of evidence that suggests that sporting spaces do elicit strong emotions (Archer and Wildman, 2021). However, I have not shared my experience with you to add to this literature. Instead, I have shared this as a personal memory based on my lived and felt experiences of this place, separate from my professional life. Other examples are found in our everyday environment.

> A completely undistinguished street of terraced houses builds up over the years a considerable symbolic potential, as though it absorbs the innumerable discharges of emotional energy released in forgotten day to day transactions. For the inhabitants of that street, the architecture and all the other urban

impediments, provide symbolic depth to life; through grimy bricks and flaming mortar the past retains the breath of life. (Smith, 1975: 77)

In the context of iconic heritage sites, we can look to the outpourings of grief attached to the fires at the Category A listed Glasgow School of Art (Figure 1) and the World Heritage Site of Notre Dame, Paris. Images of people gathering to mourn the loss of these buildings and process their grief circulated through global media outlets. The fact that so many people stood in shock, cried uncontrollable tears, and then waged a fraught battle over the most appropriate ways to reconstruct these two buildings demonstrated that, for these people, these two historic places mattered emotionally. If we put these examples alongside the stadium and the terraced houses, we can see that 'historic' can include places that are both officially designated as listed buildings or in conservation areas as well as those that are unlisted.

Throughout this Element, you will read about many different historic places, but my hope is that you can filter them through and/or add in your own emotional relationships that you have with your places. You may instead recall the clock under which social rendezvous were made, the cafe in which lunch was shared, the bingo hall in which fortunes were won and lost, or the high street that shaped weekend rhythms and rituals. Some of these relationships remain hidden and highly personal while others are revealed across cultural genres. For example, Wordsworth's poems reveal his emotional relationship with the Lake District, the sights, sounds, and smells of Salford are conveyed through the song lyrics in 'Dirty Old Town', while the lived and felt reality of life in Rome comes through the films of Pier Paolo Pasolini and Federico Fellini. Emotion, and our emotional relationships with places, is therefore omnipresent and inescapable. It rests in our memories and experiences, it is in the news bulletins that flash up in front of us, the poems we read, the music we listen to, the films we watch, the streets we walk down, the buildings we visit, and the green spaces we relax in. Yet we rarely question why these emotional relationships between us and our places occur. In fact, with a few obvious exceptions (Lowenthal and Binney, 1981; Lowenthal, 2013; Page, 2016; Mayes, 2018), we have, in a Western context, rarely questioned why we conserve historic places, believing as Ashworth did, that the 'why ask "why" question is improper'. Rather, the retention of historic buildings is seen as a 'self-evident contribution to the betterment of this and future generations' (Ashworth, 1997: 95). Instead, we have turned to quantifying the economic and social value of historic places, most notably in the United Kingdom through the Heritage Counts series produced by Historic England and

Why Historic Places Matter Emotionally

Figure 1 View showing the fire damaged south-west corner of the Mackintosh Building.
Source: Canmore, Historic Environment Scotland: DP 189507 © Crown Copyright: HES. All Rights Reserved.

internationally through a series of reports produced by the Getty Institute. I suggest therefore that within this continual need to demonstrate the values of heritage we have perhaps lost sight of why historic places matter at a deeper level. As such, this Element asks the 'why' question.

Exploring Emotion

The evidence informing this Element is drawn from a four-year research project which used emoji workshops, place-based oral histories, and extant material such as planning documents, heritage policies, press releases, and a series of reports designed to prevent the loss of historic urban places to explore why historic places matter emotionally. This data covered urban areas in England and Scotland since 1975 and was collected with a clear focus on accessing the emotional dimensions of historic urban places.[1]

Emotion was built into the research design in three main ways. First, by focusing on urban change. Second, the sources and methods for data collection were chosen to prioritise emotions. Third, emotion was coded in the data analysis.

Urban Change

Urban change was used as a mechanism through which emotion would be revealed. This was based on the belief that 'so long as there is no suggestion of change, no perception of threat' then the meanings invested in a place 'tend to remain implicit and unexpressed' (Miller, 2003: 29). This view was supported by English Heritage (2008: 32), which stated that the 'social values of place ... may only be articulated when the future of a place is threatened'. In line with this thinking, three distinct types of urban change were examined.

First, the Element engages with the consequences of urban renewal for historic places within English cities in the latter decades of the twentieth century. This period was marked by sustained campaigns to prevent the demolition of historic places across Europe and the UK, as demonstrated by the inception of European Architectural Heritage Year and SAVE Britain's Heritage, both in 1975. SAVE was founded 'by a group of planners, architects and journalists in reaction to the destruction of historic buildings, with the clear sense that their concern was shared by the wider public, and that the press could be encouraged to articulate this concern' (Wilkinson, 2006: 108). This focus on preventing demolition is primarily demonstrated by a linguistic and thematic analysis of published reports by SAVE Britain's Heritage in the 1970s and 1980s in the capital city of London along with Bradford, Burnley, Gateshead,

---

[1] The project that these findings sit within was funded by the Arts and Humanities Research Council (Grant Reference: AH/P007058/1). The work was supported by three project partners: Historic Environment Scotland, "the lead public body set up to investigate, care for and promote Scotland's historic environment" (https://www.historicenvironment.scot/about-us/); Montagu Evans LLP, "an independent property consultancy owned and run by a group of partners" (https://www.montagu-evans.co.uk/about/) and SAVE Britain's Heritage, "campaigns to bring new life to threatened historic buildings of all types and ages" (https://www.savebritainsheritage.org/about)

Halifax, Leeds, Liverpool, Manchester, and Newcastle. Each of these northern cities were suffering from decay and decline of the historic environment along with the socio-economic impacts of deindustrialisation.

Second, the Element covers the switch to heritage-led regeneration schemes co-ordinated by the public sector during the first two decades of the twenty-first century. This was achieved by exploring Historic Environment Scotland's Conservation Area Regeneration Scheme (CARS), which ran from 2007 to 2025 and provided a 'grant of up to £2 million to support cohesive heritage-focused community and economic growth projects within Conservation Areas across Scotland'. In addition, CARS was expected to

> deliver a combination of larger building repair projects, small third-party grant schemes providing funding for repairs to properties in private ownership, activities that promote community engagement with the local heritage and training for professionals in traditional building skills, all of which will contribute to sustainable economic and community development within the Conservation Area[2].

Here, the evidence is primarily drawn from emoji workshops held with local residents in the historic towns of Campbeltown, Kirriemuir, Paisley, Rothesay, and Selkirk in Scotland. Each area contains a significant number of listed buildings relative to population size, suffered from decay and decline in the historic environment, and received CARS funding between 2007 and 2022.

Third, the Element covers the role of private-sector-led regeneration of historic places in the first two decades of the twenty-first century. This is primarily demonstrated through the analysis of place-based oral histories and extant planning documents concerning the masterplan-led regeneration of the former Royal Infirmary site in Edinburgh, located within the boundaries of the Edinburgh World Heritage Site. The nineteen-acre site is now a mixed-use development called Quartermile and includes a mix of listed buildings and new buildings.

Together there are three types of urban change in fifteen places across England and Scotland including two capital cities, eight cities, and five smaller urban areas. As such, it is possible to analyse the ways in which different types of urban change affect the ways in which people across England and Scotland express why historic places matter emotionally to them.

Sources and Methods

The sources and methods for data collection were chosen to prioritise emotions. This was achieved both through extant and newly created data. The extant data was

---

[2] https://www.historicenvironment.scot/grants-and-funding/our-grants/previous-programmes/conservation-area-regeneration-scheme-cars/

mainly comprised of planning documents along with publications by SAVE Britain's Heritage. Most notably, eleven reports that focused on threatened historic places across the north of England and in London. Following the theory of 'urban change' just outlined, these reports were chosen for temporal and spatial reasons. These reports were written over a seven-year period right at the start of SAVE's existence (1979–86) when pressure to demolish historic places was acute, due to a combination of socio-economic factors including deindustrialisation, depopulation, obsolescence, and market forces. The reports were one of the 'main weapons in the SAVE armoury' (Wilkinson, 2006: 108) and were designed to both document threats to existing buildings and to provide alternative options for re-using historic buildings. As such, these reports outline both the process of preventing demolition and the emotional impacts of the perception and reality of loss. In addition, these reports were written in situ from SAVE's two offices, one in the North of England and one in London, to ensure that the authors were connecting local issues to broader national campaigns. Together, this material provides an insight into how the threat and reality of demolition reveals why these places matter emotionally.

In addition to this extant material, new data was created through adaptations of oral histories and focus group methods. The method of oral histories was adapted to focus on place and profession (Trower, 2011). As such, place-based oral histories, lasting on average one hour, with built environment professionals working across the urban development cycle in England and Scotland, were conducted. These oral histories focused on emotion and change over the career of built environment professionals and included both a focused case study (Quartermile, Edinburgh) and others that concentrated on place-based development in general across England and Scotland. The material produced by built environment professionals was complemented with the voices and feelings of residents within smaller urban areas in Scotland through adapting the traditional focus group method into emoji workshops. This method developed from an earlier photo-elicitation method (Madgin et al., 2016) as it incorporated emojis alongside photos and maps of historic places. A fuller description of the methodological approach can be found in a collection dedicated to innovative methods for place attachment (Madgin and Lesh, 2021).[3] The key points are outlined here. Six workshops were held and were comprised of four parts:

1. Photo-emoji elicitation: images of historic places were accompanied by seven responses: ☺ = happy; ☺ = very happy; ☹ = sad; ☹ = very sad; ✳

---

[3] Discussions about Campbeltown, Kirriemuir, Paisley, Rothesay and Selkirk reference the views of local residents from the emoji workshops. All other referenced data is either from extant material and cited as such or interviews with built environment professionals. Participants are referred to by pseudonym.

= angry; 😠 = furious; 😐 = neutral. Residents were asked 'when I see this building/place I feel . . . ' and then asked to click the button on an electronic response pad that most closely corresponded with their feelings (e.g. button 1 for 🙂 = happy).
2. Historic maps: participants used post-it notes and emoji stickers to convey their feelings about places they chose on the maps
3. Aerial photos: participants used post-it notes and emoji stickers to convey their feelings about places they chose on the maps
4. 'Do-it-yourself' plaques: participants were given blank blue plaques and asked to identify anything they felt was important to them and populate with emojis.

Across each of the four methods, local residents were asked to respond to how historic urban places made them feel individually and then collectively by discussing their different emojis with the rest of the group. The point of using emojis was not to elicit statistically significant quantitative data. Whether 90 per cent of participants stated that they felt 'happy' in relation to a particular place was not the focus of the workshops, which lasted, on average, two hours. Instead, the emojis stimulated long and expansive discussions about why people had chosen their emojis, contextual data about the look, feel, and use of place, and saw rich conversations between participants, which drove to the heart of why their places mattered to them emotionally.

Data Analysis

Finally, emotion was coded in the data analysis. This was achieved by adopting a linguistic and thematic analysis of a range of different sources including extant material such as planning documents, press releases, reflective texts, and reports, primarily written by SAVE Britain's Heritage in the 1970s, 1980s, and 1990s, along with the newly created material (i.e. the transcripts of place-based oral histories and emoji workshops). This included privileging the presence of emotion in the voices of the participants by analysing the emotion words either spoken by local residents and built environment professionals or written in existing documents. Through this, their emotional registers were evident. However, emotion is often downplayed and often absent from much of the rhetoric around historic urban places. As such, the material was also analysed thematically and placed into conversation with actions. In line with Sara Ahmed's (2014) question 'What Do Emotions Do?', the analysis focuses not just on what is said/written but how this is tied to decision-making in the urban environment. The approach taken was to consider how emotion is expressed through both words and actions and therefore the ways in and extent to which emotion is considered within place-based decision-making.

Alongside these approaches, a range of other sources including grey literature relevant to planning and conservation including such as international charters, national planning frameworks, national conservation guidelines, conservation area appraisals, published local history sources, and wider secondary literature were read to provide contextual data and connect to wider debates and policies. The analysis of this material forms the basis for a conceptual framework that can support an understanding of why historic urban places matter emotionally. This conceptual framework is comprised of three interlocking parts: (1) emotional responses, (2) emotional attachments, and (3) emotional communities. This framework suggests that we can understand why historic urban places matter emotionally by exploring the range of responses they provoke, the intensity of attachments they stimulate, and the types of different communities that develop a shared emotional register.

Emotion, Place, and Heritage

Understanding emotion requires shifting our thinking from seeing heritage as the historic environment to instead seeing heritage as historic places. This is not just a semantic shift. Instead, it builds from a substantial body of place-based work from across a range of disciplines that states that people and place are connected through meaning and emotion (Tuan, 1977; Altman and Low, 1992; Relph, 2008; Manzo and Devine-Wright, 2021). Yi Fu Tuan, one of the earliest exponents of this view, believed that 'the emotion felt among human beings finds expression and anchorage in things and places' (Tuan, 1979: 417). The term 'place' is therefore deliberately used in this Element to emphasise the connection between the physical and the emotional. There are innumerable definitions of place, with debates found across a number of different disciplines concerning what place is, how it differs from space, and placelessness/non-place (Cresswell, 2014). Ultimately, these definitions can be summarised as having three main elements: (1) geographic location, (2) material form, and (3) centre of meaning and value (Gieryn, 2000: 464–5). These three elements are mutually reinforcing and cannot be separated: one is not more important than the other but rather they work together, and they involve tangible forms (e.g. buildings and streets) and intangible elements (e.g. memories, symbols, rhythms, routines, and rituals). The first and second points of Gieryn's definition are well understood within heritage theory and practice. Listed buildings and conservation areas are geographic locations with material form and these aspects of the definition are therefore enshrined in the laws, policies, and practices of heritage designation and management. The third point (meaning and value) is much more complex. While values are the underpinning framework of cultural significance, it is less clear how meaning is constructed and considered within decision-making. As such, it is this latter aspect that the Element is concerned with. This is achieved by focusing on how emotion can help us understand why historic places hold meaning and therefore matter to people.

For the purposes of this Element, meaning and therefore our emotional relationships are derived through a person's interaction with, and lived and felt experiences of, historic urban places, which include designated and non-designated places. In this understanding, historic places do not have intrinsic meaning but rather meanings are constructed through individual and collective experience and therefore are historically and culturally contingent. Meaning is therefore plural and contested, not singular and agreed, it is fluid and changes over time and between space, and it differs between people. Crucially, in this understanding, meaning cannot occur without an emotional relationship between people and place.

In developing this view, this Element engages with key themes in critical heritage studies. In particular, it is situated within an increasing body of academic work that explores the emotional dimensions of heritage sites, including rural and urban areas and museum/visitor attractions (Byrne and Nugent, 2004; Harrison, 2004; Graham et al., 2009; Gregory, 2015; Tolia-Kelly, Waterton, and Watson, 2017; Smith, 2020; Wells, 2020; Wang, 2023). This work has started to develop an understanding of emotion and moved us from a point whereby emotion was previously believed to be the 'elephant in the room of heritage and museum studies' (Smith and Campbell, 2015: 443) to something that is actively engaged with in theory and practice. Within this emerging work there is a desire to develop empirical evidence through using innovative methods that directly focus on emotion in both data collection and analysis (Madgin and Lesh, 2021). Emerging work in the field of heritage and emotion is also opening up powerful new lines of enquiry based on different theoretical positions. For example, Smith, Campbell, and Wetherall's (2018) use of 'affective practices' sits alongside the more-than-representational approaches taken by Tolia-Kelly, Waterton, and Watson (2017). This Element positions itself within this tradition and trajectory of scholarship by using original empirical evidence to critically analyse how we can understand emotion. To achieve this, it draws on insights and literatures both from within and outwith critical heritage studies, and particularly from environmental psychology and humanistic geography, to develop a framework that concentrates on three key components of emotion: responses, attachments, and communities.

In line with more recent attempts within critical heritage studies to align theories and practices, the Element is also located within the development of people-centred approaches to both heritage and planning. In a heritage context, this approach has evolved from more traditional theories of heritage conservation, which ascribed value based on the primacy of an expert view of physical fabric. This traditional approach, while retaining its primacy, is continually being refined through the introduction since the 1960s of concepts including 'sense/spirit of place', 'genius loci', 'townscape', and 'character'. Each of these concepts reflected a desire to try to isolate and understand the meaning of place by both including and going beyond built fabric (Jivén and Larkham, 2003; Schofield and Szymanski, 2010; Bandarin and van Oers, 2012).

Into the twenty-first century, policies and practices further developed the linguistic canon by using words that more explicitly linked people and place. Historic Environment Scotland, 'the lead public body set up to investigate, care for and promote Scotland's historic environment'[4], outlined their more people-centred approach in their revised definition of the Scottish historic environment as 'the physical evidence for human activity that connects people with place, linked with the associations we can see, feel and understand' (Scottish Government, 2014: 2). This linguistic shift was also supported by initiatives such as *What's Your Heritage?* (2017) and a change to include Social and Historical Interest in the revised guidance for selection and designation (2019) – each of which were designed to centre people more formally within an evolving heritage system. This is paralleled in England, as demonstrated by a raft of more people-centred measures inaugurated by Historic England, 'the public body that helps people care for, enjoy and celebrate England's spectacular historic environment'[5], through their introduction of communal and social value in their six *Conservation Principles*, which are intended to guide change according to best practice. For example, the Principle for Communal/Social Value recognises some places 'may have fulfilled a community function that has generated a deeper attachment' (Historic England, 2008: 32). However, while spaces have opened up for more people to become involved in heritage decisions, social value – the principle most dedicated to people–place relations – still remains marginalised (Jones, 2017) and understandings of emotion remain under-developed.

In a planning context, spaces for people to participate increasingly opened up, as exemplified by *People and Planning*, the report of the Committee on Public Participation in Planning, commonly known as the *Skeffington Report* (1968). This approach developed in the twenty-first century through a range of initiatives including the Community Empowerment Act in Scotland (2015), Assets of Community Value (Department for Communities and Local Government, 2011), and the introduction of Neighbourhood Plans brought in under the Localism Act (2011)[6], which have each been used to support a more

---

[4] www.historicenvironment.scot/about-us/   [5] https://historicengland.org.uk/about/what-we-do/
[6] www.legislation.gov.uk/ukpga/2011/20/contents/2011-11-15

people-centred approach to planning. This was paralleled by the definition of the historic environment in the National Planning Policy Framework in England as 'all aspects of the environment resulting from the interaction between people and places through time, including all surviving physical remains of past human activity, whether visible, buried or submerged, and landscaped and planted or managed flora' (Department of Levelling Up, Housing and Communities, 2023: 68). The extent to which planning has truly evolved into being 'people-centred' though remains contested (Inch et al., 2019).

These moves at a national level do not sit within a vacuum, and arguably much of this discourse has been shaped by international practices. For example, the place-based approach of the Australian *Burra Charter* (1979), particularly through its revised versions (1999 and 2013), was seen as a necessary way to broaden the definition of cultural significance by seemingly bringing in a more people-centred view of heritage, although how far this went is debatable (Waterton et al., 2006). This approach was further extended through other key declarations and conventions, most notably the *Nara Document on Authenticity* (ICOMOS, 1994) and the *Convention on the Value of Cultural Heritage for Society* (*Faro Convention*; Council of Europe, 2005).

Together, this produces a substantial heritage and planning lexicon that hints at people–place relations as 'association', 'attachment', 'interaction', and 'connection' sit alongside other terms such as 'sense/spirit of place', '*genius loci*', 'townscape', 'character', 'social value', 'communal value', and 'social historical interest'. It is thus undeniable that both the heritage and planning sector are aware of the relationship between people and place but arguably there is still very little understanding of what this relationship is comprised of, far less the emotional aspects of these relationships, or put differently, why historic places matter emotionally. This translates into a recognition within heritage organisations that things need to be done differently. For example, Historic Environment Scotland (2017) stated, 'We think that people are increasingly interested in different aspects of our history that our listing and designation policies have not traditionally recognised' (7). This Element provides a significant entry point into these issues by providing a conceptual framework that enables us to understand why historic urban places matter emotionally and how emotion, in the form of responses, attachments, and communities affects decision-making in the urban environment.

Emotion within Place-Based Decision-Making

Emotion has been largely neglected within decision-making in both the traditional and people-centred approaches to heritage and planning. This is largely a product of history, given that there remains an entrenched mistrust of the role of emotion within decision making in the Western world. Historically, a desire for rationality and an unwavering belief in objectivity resulted in a mindset that neglected or even outright rejected emotion within decision-making. This Element refutes this position to instead see 'emotion' as a valid category of information. As such, the underpinning assumption in the Element is that emotional responses, attachments, and communities, are valid forms of evidence that help us to better understand people's relationships with historic urban places and therefore, in the words of Historic England, enables us to develop 'a better understanding of how heritage is meaningful to people in their everyday surroundings and why they engage with or feel excluded from their heritage'[7].

A mistrust of emotion is a fundamental part of the Authorised Heritage Discourse (AHD), which remains central to heritage decision-making (Smith, 2006). Smith argues that 'emotional or subjective activity' is not acknowledged within the AHD as it instead favoured 'facts', 'remembrance', or 'commemoration' (58). This is evident as early as the origins of the formal conservation movement, as seen in the parliamentary debates for the original Ancient Monuments Act, eventually passed in 1882. Here, one protagonist rejected emotion as 'he trusted that the House would look at the subject from a business, and not from a sentimental point of view' (HC Deb, 14 April 1875: cc905). Here, emotion is seen as unhelpful within the confines of an emerging process-driven system based on objective rules and regulations. This is supported in the allied practice of town and country planning, where there are strong parallels with the AHD. Hoch (2006), for example, noted that planners/analysts rarely recognise emotions and indeed 'learn to treat emotions as a source of bias and distortion' (367). Baum (2015) built on this by finding that planners 'largely resist recognising emotion' because 'Western culture downplays the role of emotion in human behaviour' (498). While this view has remained dominant, it is possible to complicate the narrative by focusing on where we can identify emotion within place-based decision-making.

One way of accessing this information is to see how heritage and emotion have been drawn together through rhetoric. For example, despite the desire to reject sentimentalism in the debates around the Ancient Monuments Act, emotion words were evident as expressed by the proposer of the bill, Sir John Lubbock.

> Under existing circumstances it had frequently happened over and over again that interesting and venerable, and in some cases sacred, monuments were destroyed, generally for very homely and trivial reasons, to be used as manure, to mend the roads, to serve as gateposts, or for other similar purposes, and when the mischief was done, everybody regretted it, and was sorry and surprised. (HC Deb, 14 April 1875: cc881)

---

[7] https://historicengland.org.uk/research/agenda/research-theme-value/

This was not an isolated incident but rather connected to other more romantic views developed in the nineteenth century, primarily by John Ruskin's evocation of the emotional power of architecture both for the producer and the receiver. In the twentieth and twenty-first centuries, we see emotion words being used by national heritage organisations, which believe that we can 'celebrate the buildings we love'[8] or that 'parts of our history ... can be painful or shameful by today's standards'[9]. Furthermore, we can also see the word 'emotion' being used explicitly within policy/practice documents. For example, Historic England's (2008) *Conservation Principles* uses the phrases 'emotional links' (8) and 'emotional impact' (10), the draft consultation document to revise the *Principles* uses 'emotional evidence' (Historic England, 2017: 56) whereas 'emotional associations' is used in *Scottish Historic Environment Policy* (Historic Scotland, 2009: 45). On an international stage, the *Québec Declaration on the Preservation of the Spirit of Place* (ICOMOS, 2008) uses the word 'emotion' in its definition of 'Spirit of Place'. In this context, it is clear that a heritage–emotion lexicon exists within professional practice. This lexicon either explicitly uses 'emotion(al)' as a term; evokes emotions through emotion words; or implicitly refers to it through terms such as 'attachment'. However, there remains little sense as to what is meant by emotional associations, links, or evidence or indeed the extent to which emotion affects place-based decision-making. This ongoing tension is perhaps best summarised by Placido Domingo, Chair of Europa Nostra, a pan 'European voice of civil society committed to safeguarding and promoting cultural and natural heritage'[10], who stated:

> Cultural Heritage is a capital of irreplaceable cultural, social, environmental and economic value. This is true for Europe, as it is for the rest of the world. We know this in our hearts and minds, but the policies and investments necessary to sustain our heritage have to be based on more than profound feelings or strong beliefs. We also need facts and figures to prove and illustrate those convictions. Articulating the value of our heritage by providing quantitative and qualitative evidence of its benefits and impacts, will indeed give more strength to the voice of cultural heritage in Europe. (CHCfE Consortium, 2015: 6)

The extent to which this lexicon of emotion drives or informs place-based decision-making is therefore under-researched. Two notable exceptions to this suggest that heritage practitioners in the United States and United Kingdom do 'gauge significance by calling on emotional forms of attunement' but that it is 'rendered invisible in the official processes' (Hoskins in Crossick and

---

[8] https://historicengland.org.uk/whats-new/features/love-letters-to-buildings
[9] https://historicengland.org.uk/whats-new/statements/contested-heritage/
[10] www.europanostra.org/our-work/

Kaszynska, 2016: 21). The most explicit use of emotion within heritage practice to date is found with the National Trust's (England and Wales) use of the concept of 'topophilia', defined as the 'love of place' as they 'set out to explore and understand this visceral but intangible feeling more deeply' (National Trust, 2017: 3). Thus, through a series of quantitative and qualitative studies, the National Trust (2019) explored the 'depths of people's neurophysiological connection with place' (11). Their work demonstrated the 'strong emotional connection between people and places' (National Trust, 2017: 5) and further suggested that 'there is a link between having a deep-rooted emotional connection to a place and having a better sense of wellbeing' (National Trust, 2019: 8). In this evolving context, it is evident that emotional relationships exist between people and historic places but emotion, as a category of information, within decision-making remains under-developed and therefore under-utilised.

Introducing the Conceptual Framework

While work on emotion is growing within critical heritage studies and is gaining increased attention with heritage practice, two key issues remain. First, we do not fully understand why historic urban places matter emotionally. Second, the role of emotion within place-based decision-making remains under-researched. To achieve better understanding of both issues, the Element sets out a conceptual framework based on three interconnecting components: responses, attachments, and communities (Table 1).

Table 1 Definitions of the terms used in the tripartite conceptual framework

Components	Definition
Emotional **responses**	The verbal, visual, and/or written expression of a particular emotion in relation to a historic urban place
Emotional **attachments**	The bonds that form between people and historic urban places
Emotional **communities**	Collectives who hold and value – or devalue – a shared set of emotional responses and attachments to historic urban places

The conceptual framework recognises that each of these three components – responses, attachments, and communities – are important in and of themselves and indeed could comprise a book on their own. As will be further developed in the introductions to the forthcoming sections, they each have significant intellectual lineages with work conducted across the arts, humanities, social, and natural sciences. However, the contention in this Element is that they are stronger when placed alongside one another. For example, while responses are the most visible aspect of our emotional relationships, and are often revealed through words and emojis, they do not, by themselves, reveal the profound attachments that we develop to historic urban places. Attachments are often hidden and sometimes only revealed during times of change and as such can be less visible than responses. However, it is possible to access and understand attachments through active listening, close reading, and thematic analysis of qualitative material. Drawing on work from within the place attachment field, which focuses on people–place relations and particularly the way that people form emotional bonds with place (Altman and Low, 1992), this Element posits that emotional attachments help us to better understand the profound nature of our emotional relationships with place. Alongside this, it is crucial to explore who is responding emotionally and forming emotional attachments. Here the book adapts historian Barbara Rosenwein's concept of emotional communities to focus on two distinct types of communities: place and practice. In essence, the framework does not seek to reduce emotion to individual responses located in emotion words and emojis but rather recognises that people form intense psycho-emotional attachments to historic places at both an individual and collective level. Together, this information provides a robust, rich, and layered understanding of why, how, and for whom historic places matter emotionally. The framework also examines the notion that emotion cannot be trusted and/or that it distorts place-based decision-making. By systematically working through how people respond and form attachments to historic urban places, we find that emotion is a valid form of information that can support place-based decision-making.

The Element develops the conceptual framework through its structure. Each section examines one aspect of the framework: responses (Section 2), attachments (Section 3), and communities (Section 4). The Element then ties the three components back together (Section 5) by exploring the ways in which, and extent to which, emotion, in the form of response, attachments, and communities, is recognised within place-based decision-making. The Element concludes by considering what the findings could mean for present and future theories and practices in the heritage sector.

2 Emotional Responses

> Battersea Power Station towers over the River Thames like a great ocean liner. You may love it or loathe it, but it is impossible to ignore it (Binney, 1981: np).

Historic urban places have the capacity to move us in stark and obvious ways, as with London's Battersea Power Station, as well as in quieter and more subtle ways. This section explores what kinds of emotional responses historic urban places provoke and why they make us feel these ways. To achieve this, the section introduces the first element of the tripartite conceptual framework, set out in Table 1: emotional responses. These responses are defined as the verbal, visual, and/or written expression of a particular emotion in relation to a historic urban place. In so doing, this section is located within key debates concerning how we define and how we capture emotional responses.

First, despite numerous classifications and categorisations of emotions (Tracey and Randles, 2011) debate remains as to what an emotion is. The 'classical' approach to 'basic' emotions based on universalism and essentialism and a belief that we each share the same emotions and responses (Ekman, 1992) is now challenged by the theory of 'constructed emotions', which instead focuses on how emotions are instead made through individualised experiences (Feldman Barrett, 2017). This section is located within this tension, as it explores a range of responses, including pride, fear, and happiness, that could be seen as 'basic' emotions. However, this does not signal a preference for the 'classical' theory of emotions but rather results from an analysis of the emotion words contained within the data. Instead, the framework suggests that the theory of constructed emotions, which is more inclusive in its understanding not just of how many emotions exist but how they originate, fit together, change, and are fundamentally shaped by historical, social, and cultural contexts (Mesquita, 2022), is more relevant to understanding emotional responses to historic urban places. This section posits that emotional responses to historic places are shaped by time, person, place, culture, and context and therefore vary between people, within place, and over time.

Second, running parallel to this debate are questions about how to access emotions. Traditionally, looking for the 'fingerprints' of basic emotions through analysing facial expressions and bodily reactions was favoured. Instead, the approach taken here is to respect the diversity of emotional expression by analysing emotional responses through words, emojis, and practices (Sheer, 2012; Frevert, 2014; Madgin, 2021e). As such, the emotional responses outlined in this section are derived from the emotion words used either by participants in the place-based oral histories with built environment professionals and emoji workshops with local residents (Madgin, 2021e) or within existing documentary sources with a focus on the place-based reports written by SAVE Britain's Heritage.

This section develops an understanding of emotional responses through a staged process. First, it isolates one emotion, pride, to try to understand what it means to the people who use the word and how it relates to historic urban places. Then, the analysis considers the blended nature of emotion reflecting the fact that emotion words were rarely offered in isolation (Israelsson et al., 2023). Finally, this section explores how responses are mixed, defined as the co-existence of positive and negative emotion words (Berios et al., 2015). For example, the potential loss of a historic urban place may provoke sadness, a conventionally negative emotion, but in fact this word was found to be related to the fear of losing the positive emotions, such as joy, experienced in the places discussed in this section. Although sadness and fear may appear to be negative, it is precisely because positive emotions such as joy exist that these supposedly obverse emotions can be expressed.

Isolating Emotions: Pride

'Pride' and in particular pride in place has been the focus of sustained attention from the UK Government (2019–24) as part of its desire to 'level up' the UK economy (Marsh et al., 2023). Despite this research being conducted before the Levelling Up White Paper (UK Government, 2021) was published, it was evident that pride was a recurring emotion word used both by built environment professionals and local residents. There were a range of reasons why pride was expressed. For example, when asked how Paisley Abbey (Figure 2), a twelfth-century church, made them feel, local residents focused on pride:

Figure 2 Paisley Abbey

Source: Canmore, Historic Environment Scotland: DP 250520 © Historic Environment Scotland. All Rights' Reserved.

Lucy: I think that's one thing in Paisley that you, if you're driving along, it stands out.
Kirstin: It makes you feel proud.
Lucy: Aye.
Various: Aye.
Kirstin: It is the one thing I think.
Interviewer: Why does it make you feel proud?
Kirstin: Because it's such a beautiful building.
Lucy: We've had it so long. right.
Kirstin: And there's not many as old as that.

The emphasis on the aesthetic, architectural, and historic value of the abbey was matched by other examples, namely SAVE writing about Temple Mill in Leeds, which was described as 'a blatant expression of the pride of John Marshall, the town's industrial superstar' (Binney, 1979: 51). Allied to this was also the loss of and lack pride that troubled SAVE as the physical structures from the industrial revolution were demolished

> Two hundred chimneys, each one of the heaven-storming symbol of the pride and prestige of the company that owned it, rose over the mass of housing and factories. The sight of these chimneys, on the rare clear day when they could be seen, must have been staggering, and it remains so even today, after the felling of over half of them (Binney, 1979: 9).

This loss of pride which paralleled the loss of the built environment was not however solely attributed to the architectural and historic interest. Rather, SAVE recognised the human dimension of loss: 'The dislocation and sense of loss can break down the pride and respect that ordinary citizens may have in their hometown. What they had identified as being their world ceases to be part of them' (Binney, 1979: 25). In these examples, pride is related to how it is used within daily life patterns as people move through places and well as the way a building looks.

Pride was also evoked in the context of working with historic urban places. In particular, pride was influenced by the intellectual, practical, and logistical challenge of working with historic places. Pride could occur at any time within the urban development process from the initial chance to work with a prominent listed building because of its historical reputation, perhaps as an example the world's first 'something', or because it is an iconic local landmark that is seen to give the town a special meaning or character, and right through to the end of the process. Built environment professional Phil spoke eloquently about pride in the course of his work. First of all, pride came from knowing that 'what you're dealing with is special' and second, pride was evident in an awareness of the degree of difficulty of working with historic buildings

> So there's lots of good things about it, but it's very challenging and I think that ... I mean it's challenging to get the labour, challenging to get the management, it's challenging to get the funding, it's challenging to get the consents, and the actual projects themselves are complex and challenging.

Third, the challenge of delivering a restored historic urban building ensured that Phil felt an 'immense sense of pride and satisfaction' on finishing the job, because 'sometimes the more challenging something is, the more sweet the success is'. This was developed further, with Phil stating, 'You can feel that you've done a good job and that you have been involved in creating something special and also created a lasting legacy, or you've continued what already is a legacy, you know?' Finally, pride was not only something that was only associated with the history of the building or in the process of change but also was seen as an emotional response that drove the nature of future change. For example, a link was made by both built environment professionals and local residents as to the relationship between pride and a desire to care for historic urban places in the future. For example, Phil went on to state:

> Heritage buildings actually help make a place and an area, and they cast some magic over an area that actually gives people pride in where they're living and actually makes them look after their area potentially more and also it then has a snowball effect and brings in more investment.

Isolating emotions in this way helps us to understand what pride means to people in particular temporal and spatial contexts and to see any continuities and changes across time and space. From this analysis, we can see that there appears to be a relationship between historic places and pride that is shaped by the domains of architecture, history, aesthetics, challenge, and legacy and comes from being in, looking at, and working with historic places.

Blending Emotions: Conventionally Positive Responses

The word 'proud' or 'pride' was often expressed alongside a number of other emotion words. For example, local residents invoked their own emotion words when creating their own 'do it yourself' heritage plaques in the emoji workshops. In one example, Penny nominated 'Campbeltown Town Hall ... surprise, surprise, purchased on behalf of the community by South Kintyre Development Trust, 2014' and used the 'happy, smiley face with the rosy cheeks' emoji. This historic place made Penny feel 'chuffed', 'pride', and 'happy'. Penny went on to say, 'We do feel very precious about it I think is the word! I feel really precious about it, and the town, but particularly with the town hall.' Feeling a sense of happiness and pride was strongly related to the community ownership of the town hall and because the building was back in everyday use.

A combination of emotional responses, including pride, love, happy, and chuffed can inform particular kinds of actions within the urban environment, namely the kinds of place protective behaviour demonstrated by the South Kintyre Development Trust, a community anchor organisation led by a board of volunteers who all lived in South Kintyre[11]. This link between emotional responses to a place and place protective behaviour, such as community ownership, can be set within a longer trajectory of the work of local and national civic amenity societies, where pride and enthusiasm has been a motivating factor both in campaigns to retain historic buildings and in the formation of societies (Craggs et al., 2016). In this way emotions are used productively to secure certain kinds of outcomes as places undergo change.

A further example of the blending of emotion words came in Campbeltown where residents, when asked how a photograph of the Picture House made them feel, responded overwhelmingly with happy or very happy, and in their explanations went on to say that pride was a contributing factor

Lee: Memories.
Isla: Pride.
Penny: It's a really cool building!
    <Laughter> . . .
Isla: It's really attractive.
Leanne: Stood the test of time, you know.
Amy: It's not just a bog-standard cinema, it's just a lovely place!
Isla: Beautiful.
Lee: It's not just that; it's the oldest purpose-built cinema in Scotland!
Amy: I don't know . . . to you . . .
Lee: To me that's pride!
Amy: I know it's pride, but I use it all the time but it's not because it's the oldest; it's because it's lovely and it's a nice space and it's doing good work and that's why I like it.
Isla: I love the Art Deco design of it!
Various: Yeah.
Isla: I sketched it once and it just looks beautiful.
Sally: I forgot it used to look like that as well, I forgot about the front like that.
Gordon: It's quite complicated 'cause it's nice to look at and it gives you things that you can do, it's a big achievement that it's been got back to its original and I think there's

---

[11] https://skdt2014.wixsite.com/skdt

a sense of pride in the history of it ... It's a whole series of different things. It makes you very happy. If it was just a picture house you go to, you're just happy!
<Laughter>

Emotions, therefore, do not often happen in isolation and so it was often difficult to separate out pride from happiness. Within this, it is clear to see that a range of factors informed the residents' emotional responses. Like with Paisley Abbey, the historical nature of the cinema was referenced, both in terms of the fact it's the 'oldest' and because of the happy memories that the participants recalled from using the cinema. The architectural style of the building was referenced with residents saying it was 'attractive' and 'beautiful'. Here we can see that the traditional and statutory categories for heritage designation – architectural and historic interest – are determining factors in producing positive emotional responses. However, these responses were also provoked by the cumulative lived and felt experiences of the residents in Paisley and Campbeltown. In these ways, the range of emotional responses were provoked by the recalled places of the past and the felt experiences of the present.

The complex and blended nature of emotional responses is perhaps best reflected by the concept of 'wow', which has not traditionally been considered as a 'basic' emotion but rather an emotional experience that is comprised of a range of interlinked emotional responses (Desmet et al., 2007). 'Wow' was evoked in a number of different ways and, as with pride and happiness, Lorraine, a built environment professional, demonstrated how the embodied experience of being in, walking around, and moving through the former Royal Infirmary in Edinburgh was important

> I guess it's about the understanding of our heritage, about understanding the buildings, and being able to enjoy them. I mean I think for the surgical block, the A listed nature of it, being able to walk into it, and see the pictures of Florence Nightingale Home, having been in the building, and then you're standing in that space ... wow, this is a bit of history to it, because it's ... the surgical block was all about the cross-ventilation from the windows and things, and that's where it came from.

'Wow' was strongly related to the ways in which this made people feel and how they looked. This is exemplified by built environment professionals Phil and Howard, who, when asked what was special about historic urban places answered:

> It's the architecture and it's the history, which is why they're actually listed buildings, 'cause they need to be of special architectural or history interest. But for me it's ... how something makes you feel ... so you can go into a building and you can go wow, you can stand outside a building and you can go wow, and you can be a landscape and you can go wow,

and the thing is that actually it makes you marvel at what people have produced in the past and it puts in perspective your ability or your place in the world, you know? (Phil).

We derive pleasure from these historic places and buildings through the things I mentioned before, human scale, sort of handmade qualities of buildings as well, obviously the later you go the less of that you get. But the fact that some of them are incredible buildings anyway, I mean if you look at a cathedral or something ... , just you know it's stunning, just to look at it ... or monumental buildings. That's kind of obvious and people are just kind of overawed by them or awed by them, Tower of London or something, wow, look at that (Howard).

Desmet and colleagues (2007) found that surprise, desire, and fascination could be incorporated into the composite emotional experience that could be defined as 'wow'. The specific emotional responses to historic urban places broadened this out to also include aesthetic appreciation, interest, awe, enjoyment, and pleasure. Of most relevance here is how Desmet and colleagues' concept of 'wow' can help us to go beyond isolating particular emotional responses, such as pride, and to think about how a range of emotional responses can co-exist. In these ways, this evidence moves us towards understanding the interactions between a number of different emotional responses, which together form a rich composite emotional experience that reflects how people feel in and about historic urban places.

Blending Emotions: Conventionally Negative Responses

Any discussion of composite emotional experiences needs to consider the ways in which more conventionally negative emotions also co-exist. This was most evident in the ways in which fear provoked other kinds of emotions, including pain, but also left a temporal legacy for people and place.

The emotional response of fear was multifaceted and related to three main areas. First, there was a recurring acknowledgment from built environment professionals that there was a complex emotional register emanating from the process of urban change. This was encapsulated by Derek's belief as follows:

There's no doubt in my mind that the impact on the existing urban environment is probably the biggest issue that we deal with, either in a positive or negative way. And sometimes that's people have a fear of change, so that's not always heritage buildings, it could be anything in the sense that if somebody's coming along and saying, 'We'd like to propose a development in this area', understandably, people who live around that area will have certain anxieties and certain fears.

This generalised fear of change expressed here can be explored in the context of emotional hangovers. In the context of industrial cities, this related to the 'shudders and pangs of guilt' caused by the polluted, insanitary conditions associated with the industrial revolution

> Hippolyte Taine's description of a northern city conveys what many have felt: 'the factories extend their flanks of fouled brick one after another, bare, with shutterless windows, the symmetrical streets seem like corpses laid out side by side'. Today this is compounded not only by memories of child labour and industrial disease and accident, but a tendency to associate anything old with the galling years of the slump – when unemployment in some mill towns reached 60 per cent. Hence the desire voiced by local councillors to erase every physical feature which could awaken such painful memories. It is a kind of subconscious fear that the buildings themselves, if allowed to continue in existence, could put the clock back and drag people back into drudgery and deprivation. (Binney, 1979: 3)

This fear was very real and was evident in the swathes of planning, welfare, and housing policies that were implemented from the inter-war years in the UK. In essence, a fear of not changing was more pervasive than the fear of change in the minds of local councillors and planners (Madgin, 2021d) whereas the fear of losing familiar environments, existing routines, and embedded social networks was felt deeply within urban communities, as recognised by SAVE:

> Demolition has often involved appalling social disruption where not only fabric but families, businesses and communities have been broken up. The pain and deprivation caused by the loss of the personal heritage of home, cherished street of familiar surroundings has been cruelly underestimated. (SAVE Britain's Heritage, 1975: 1289)

This large-scale demolition of the existing environment left a deep emotional legacy that went beyond momentary fear and pain. Built environment professionals Christopher and Aaron reflected on this in the context of new development: 'In the sixties and seventies, we put up very high buildings, and so people were right to be worried because they could see ... that there was no ... the new buildings didn't have a relationship to what the place was (Christopher).' This type of 'regrettable ... post-war thinking' that resulted in 'cheerless, uniform, uninviting' and remained 'unpeopled and unloved' (Wood et al., 1983: 3) left an emotional scar in place and over time that affected future phases of urban change.

Now, the unfortunate thing for that is we inherit those views because people are very, very suspicious and they'd sooner have something that at least they know, like or understand, rather than have it all swept away and replaced with something new. So in all situations like this, even when they're less emotionally connected, you've got a lot of hearts and minds to win around because you've got to be demonstrating to people all the time, you haven't just come, you're gonna change things, because you have to change, you're going to change it for the better, you have to believe that otherwise there's no point doing it and you have to show people that the way that architecture can work, the way it can make places, the way it can make buildings, can respond to historic context and local context in a smart way (Aaron).

Common to these blended responses was thus a complex temporal as well as spatial register. Often the perception of the future was reflected through the memories of what had happened in the past. As such, these emotions were provoked by present-day worries and imagined concerns based on recalled memories. These more conventionally negative responses were therefore not static and provoked solely by present-day circumstances but were infused by a complex set of temporally and spatially derived factors.

Mixing Emotions

Local residents and built environment professionals did not just express conventionally positive or negative emotional response in isolation. Instead, both types of responses were evident. This was most evident in the use of the term 'sublime' as well as within discussion of the use of scaffolding within heritage-led regeneration initiatives. SAVE adopted the concept of the 'sublime' when discussing vast industrial complexes such as the Yorkshire Mills that 'still impress, by their size and even grandeur. Few people would call them beautiful, fewer still picturesque. They are instead what the 18th century called sublime' (Binney, 1979: 4). Contained within this was a belief that mills contained Burke's qualities of 'Obscurity, Power, Privations, Vastness, Infinity, Succession and Uniformity, all qualities which combine to induce a sense of awe, or ultimately of terror, in the onlooker' (Binney, 1979: 4). Here, it is clear that there are a set of mixed reactions to the visual dominance of industrial buildings. On the one hand, they are a source of pride and awe but also invoke fear, guilt, and/or terror.

In Campbeltown, buildings that once made people feel happy, they enjoyed using, and had fond memories of became suffused with conventionally negative emotional responses: 'I have friends coming . . . and then before they came I was going, "Ah . . . it's . . . building that is boarded up and I thought oh, . . . where am

I gonna take them?" I felt embarrassed' (Sally). This conventionally negative response was in spite of the fact that residents recognised that putting up scaffolding was a necessary, if unpleasant, aspect of development. As Isla recalled, 'It was good because it was progression, there was stuff happening, but everything was so ugly and depressing.' In addition, the scaffolding still provoked conventionally negative emotional responses even when mitigating steps were taken by the developers. Here, Gordon remarked on how being in and moving through the historic urban place generated a negative emotional response

> The actual building, to walk past that was pretty sad. Even when it was getting done up, because the company that did it came in and did it, ... they put attractive hoarding round the front and that helped a bit, but ... yeah, that was a bit sad to watch.

This point was replicated in Selkirk (Figure 3) as the impact of the scaffolding on the clock tower was felt in residents' everyday lives, as recalled by Logan: 'Well I'm happy it's been refurbished, because for a long time it was covered in scaffolding, and number of times you walk along the town and look up to see what time it is and the clock wasnae there!'

Here, it is apparent that everyday lived and felt experiences of historic urban places produce a mix of conventionally positive and negative responses. The exact nature of this mix is heavily dependent on the ways in which our everyday experiences are disrupted by the process of urban change. As such, isolating emotions can only lead us so far. We may be able to interrogate pride or fear, but we cannot divorce them from the range of other emotional responses that are inextricably bound up within the emotional register of historic urban places: an emotional hangover from the 1960s does not just produce fear but also anxiety, worry, regret, pain, and suspicion with short and long-term consequences for people and place. Isolating and combining emotional responses and seeing them as part of composite emotional experiences based on place and time is therefore crucial to developing an understanding of why historic places matter emotionally to people.

Conclusion

We know that historic urban places matter emotionally because they have the capacity to provoke different kinds of emotional responses. In this section alone, twenty-one responses were expressed and were mixed between conventionally positive and negative (see Figure 4).

Figure 3 Selkirk clock tower
Source: Canmore, Historic Environment Scotland: SC 336438 © Crown Copyright: HES. All Rights' Reserved.

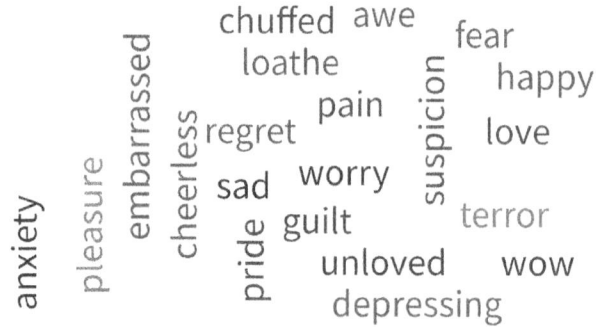

Figure 4 Emotion words used in this section
Source: mentimeter.com. All Rights' Reserved.

The plural, rich, and complex emotional register outlined in this section arose from a number of recurring themes. First, it is undeniable that the architectural and historic characteristics of the places are influential in the expression of emotional responses. This ranged from the conventionally positive words associated with the beauty of Paisley Abbey and also the 'oldest purpose-built cinema' in Campbeltown to the conventionally negative words associated with the 'regrettable' post-Second World War replacement buildings. Architectural and historic interest were therefore key in the expression of emotion words.

Second, the everyday lived and felt experiences of the historic urban place were crucial in the formation of a person's emotional responses. From the impact of scaffolding to the use of the Picture House, the ways in which people lived their daily lives in place conditioned their use of emotion words. Not being able to see the clock on the clock tower and/or not being able to show friends and visitors around the parts of the town that matter to you co-existed alongside cumulative visits to the Picture House or driving past the abbey in stimulating conventionally positive emotions.

Third, working with historic urban places was also a powerful generator of emotional responses. These could be seen throughout the urban development process including working with special places, securing consents, and the enjoyment of finishing the job. Working directly with historic urban places provoked a range of emotional responses including pleasure and pride in built environment professionals but also an awareness that their work had to be cognisant of emotional responses held by others.

Examining emotional responses to historic urban places tells us a lot about the ways people express their own feelings about places and the ways in which architectural and historic interest and people's lived, felt, and worked experiences frame emotional registers. A close reading of emotional responses also reminds us that emotions do not happen in isolation, that we can rarely, if ever, separate pride or fear for example from other types of emotions, positive or negative. However, emotional responses cannot, on their own, tell us whether our emotional relationships are volatile, fleeting, 'in the moment' feelings or the product of a deeper, more profound connection to historic urban places. Indeed, we need to 'distinguish between the *primary experience* of place which triggers an immediate, emotional and unreflective response, and the more reflective processes which, over time, lead to attachment' (Johnston, 1992: 12). Attachment is the subject of the next section and the second component of why historic places matter emotionally.

3 Emotional Attachments

> I feel that the town (Kirriemuir) is my anchor. I feel that very, very strongly. I go around when I'm out in the town every day and I look at the buildings and I think how lucky we are to live in such a lovely town. The buildings are simply beautiful (Molly).

This section introduces the second component of the conceptual framework – emotional attachments – and in particular asks how we come to see historic places as 'anchors'. More specifically, the section examines how attachments are formed and disrupted and the way we can understand differing intensities of attachment. In so doing, this section highlights how we can develop an understanding of a more profound emotional engagement with historic urban places. It therefore connects with a substantial body of work across philosophy, environmental psychology, and geography in which place is seen to be existentially important: our lives are not just shaped by place but instead we need places in order to have meaningful and fulfilled lives:

> Distinctive and diverse places are manifestations of a deeply felt involvement with those places by the people who live in them, and that for many such a profound attachment to place is as necessary and significant as a close relationship with other people (Relph, 2008: preface).

Relph's work leads us into a key tension within place-based literature – the extent to which place attachment is motivated by social and/or physical characteristics. Stedman (2003), for example, questioned the social bias of place attachment research by foregrounding the importance of physical characteristics. This imbalance between physical and social is reversed within a UK heritage context in which understandings of the physical dimensions of tangible heritage have traditionally been prioritised over social and intangible dimensions. However, this section builds from earlier work to posit that attachments to historic places are instead situated between the physical and the social (Madgin et al., 2016). In this understanding, the lens of attachment neither privileges the physical or the social but rather centres the relationship between place and person and thus collapses the divide between tangible and intangible heritage. This is achieved by considering the existential meaning of historic urban places as situated in both the existence of the physical fabric and in the everyday experiences that occur within these physical spaces. This combination gives rise to layered lived and felt experiences comprised of everyday rhythms and routines that ingrain memories, stories, and symbols in place. By considering both the existential and the everyday, the intention is to convey that attachments are not static but rather are dynamic and the focus in the section is therefore on 'forming' and 'disrupting' attachments of varying intensities rather than seeing them as fixed in place and person. Crucial to this is an awareness of the importance of the temporal horizons of attachment. Historic places bring a depth of time rooted in their permanence (existential) and their familiarity (everyday) and so past and present cannot be disconnected. However, this time depth also extends into the future given that historic places have been and will continue to be an inescapable aspect of daily life in urban Britain. How we sustain attachments across time and in place is therefore crucial to nurturing both a sense of self and a sense of place.

Forming Attachments

The need to form attachments to place can be considered through the lens of ontological security, defined as 'the confidence that most human beings have in the continuity of their self-identity and the constancy of the surrounding social and material environments of action' (Giddens, 1990: 2). This theme was developed in a heritage context by Jane Grenville (2007; 2015), who explored how our ontological security is affected through external shocks such as war or financial crises. This section takes up this theme by examining the ways in which historic urban places can support ontological security through their permanence. For example, built environment professionals demonstrated an acute awareness of the ways in which particular kinds of buildings can provide

> some continuity and familiarity and a nostalgic, warm, fuzzy feeling that there is something which has a permanence to it or has a reference back to their childhood. I think if you can retain and enhance and encapsulate that in something you do, that feels like that is a really positive thing. (Grace)

Mark and Callum considered permanence through the lens of security: 'I think we all need to feel secure in our lives and the built environment is part of that feeling of security. You need to know that when you leave your house it is going to look like it did yesterday' (Mark). Callum went deeper to discuss the materiality of historic place and how buildings, new and old, were designed to provide that subliminal sense of security and permanence: 'And I think there's evidence that some of the oldest medieval cathedrals put too much structure in for the psychological sense that it's not gonna fall down on my head.' Allied to this was a belief that familiarity was important to why historic urban places matter:

> But I think the old buildings mean that people feel that they can come here because some of it is familiar . . . . There's something of what it always has been and what we know and knew, and therefore it's safer, more acceptable, to come in. (Christopher)

> It's repetition, recognition, familiarity, safety, all those sorts of things. And there can be some icons within that, so a church with a steeple is a very familiar thing, it becomes the oldest building in a certain place, quite often, and it goes back through generations, and it has its own history and stories. (Callum)

Pubs, alongside churches, have long been a locus of attachment as demonstrated by the number of campaigns to prevent their loss. For example, SAVE teamed up with The Campaign for Real Ale (CAMRA) in 1983, as they realised that pubs were under threat from urban redevelopment and that 'the surviving pubs of redeveloped city centres and inner-city areas remain as anchors in a shattered environment' (Binney and Milne, 1983: 30). In addition to this, their joint publication recognised that 'the buildings themselves often give a sense of security in our changing times' (1983: 31). This sense of permanence and familiarity was paralleled by a focus on comfort and calm. Built environment professional Brian, for example, discussed this with reference to street lighting by eloquently considering why comfort and familiarity and history could go together:

> And there's something more comforting about things that are old and familiar, I guess? So maybe my children won't be having the same conversation <laughs> as me, but it's really what you're used to and ... Somehow I think there's something very ... going back to looking at the gas lighting that you get in Mayfair at night, you know, the warmth that you get from that kind of lighting, as opposed to modern, LED streetlights, which are all very efficient but maybe it's just a sentimental feeling, I don't know why it's better, but it's ... It links you back to the past, it makes you feel like you're slightly going back in time in a good way.

This was complemented by the belief from Callum, a built environment professional, that historic urban places could calm our senses:

> So, I think a great place will always have some sense of protection and in order for your senses to be calm and perhaps then you're engaging with whatever it is that you're looking at or enjoying your conversation to a much greater degree because there isn't some fundamental worries it's gonna fall on top of you or whatever else.

In terms of local residents, Paisley Abbey was felt to be a restorative place and as such part of their daily rhythms and routines. Annabel remembered coming 'out of the town centre, busy, people, traffic, and then you come to this small oasis of calm, and it has that about it'. Annabel went further to state that 'it's a kind of lowering the blood pressure kind of place'. Remembering how familiar places made you feel is of importance here and shows how memory and feeling can translate into a deeper emotional relationship. This was demonstrated in Campbeltown as Isla believed that 'the people have got ownership of the Picture House because they have memories about it, and they grew up and they went to it'. This familiarity generated by particular types of felt experiences, in this case the calm felt by being in and around the Abbey and also by sedimenting memories in place through repeated use, saw people develop a sense of felt ownership of place that signals something deeper than just enjoyment of place and closer to an attachment to place.

These psycho-emotional states of comfort, safety, security, and ownership provoked by our layered lived and felt experiences in place are the reason historic urban places can stimulate attachments. They demonstrate our relationship to something deeper and more enduring. Historic buildings collect layers upon layers of stories, experiences, and memories which over time produce, in Callum's words a 'sense of belonging' and an 'affiliation'. Callum went on to say, 'They, by definition, have authenticity 'cause they exist over time and there's a familiarity with that that makes us feel an affiliation, whether it be civic or communion, pub or schools or just stories, so it's thick with that.' Whether the terms used are ownership (Isla) or belonging (Callum), it is clear that the constancy of the material environment and its capacity to generate everyday experiences is crucial in the formation of emotional attachments.

Within this context, we can identify a number of different aspects of historic urban places that people form attachments to. These are summarised in the animation in Video 1 and are comprised of a number of interlocking parts. Crucially, these variables both include and go beyond the architectural and historic value of built heritage to also recognise intangible aspects of historic urban places. Some of these parts would be recognised within the traditional approach to heritage conservation that validates built fabric whereas others are more akin to the people-centred approach as they reveal how everyday experiences in place affect the formation of attachment. What is crucial within this is that ongoing heritage management initiatives, be they designation, listed building consent, and/or changes to the setting of historic places need to be cognisant of the emotional value of these places beyond their tangible existence. They are not just static memorials to a valued past but rather they are part of the fluid continuum of everyday lives, shaping stories, memories, and future meanings and it is because of both that people can form emotional attachments that in turn help to nourish their sense of self and a sense of place.

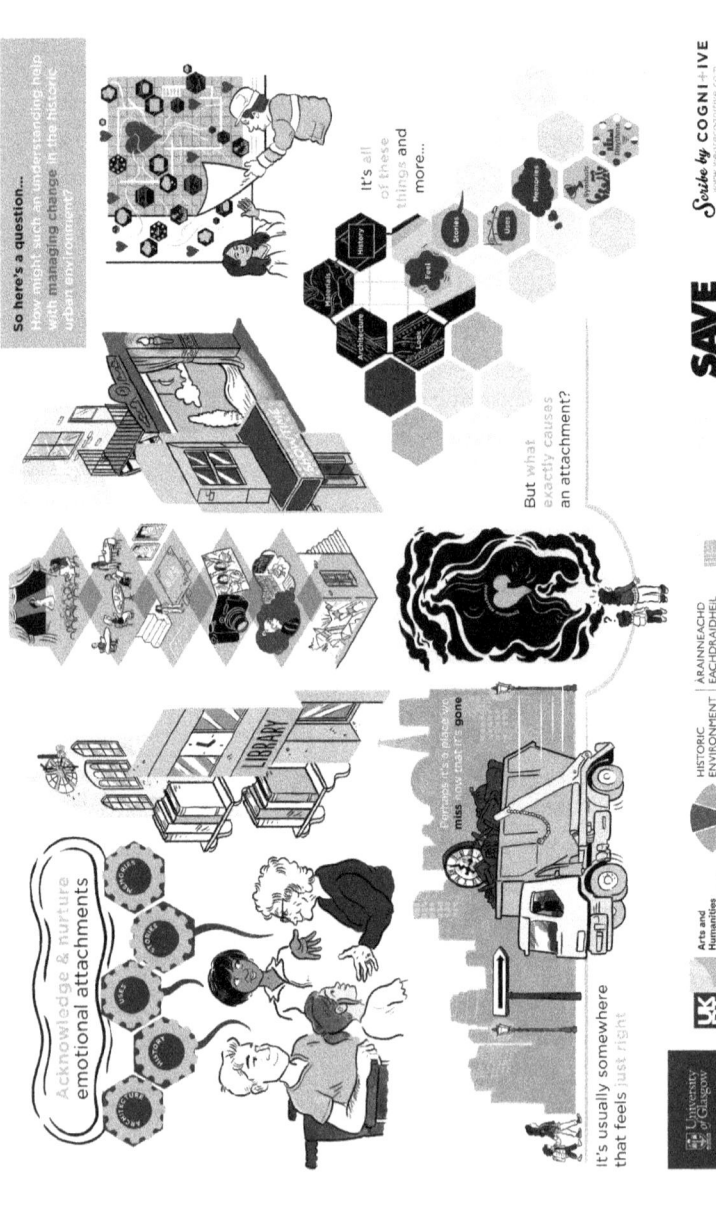

Video 1 Why People Form Emotional Attachments to Historic Urban Places. Video file and transcript available at www.cambridge.org/historicplaces

Source: We Are Cognitive (Madgin, 2021b). All Rights' Reserved.

Disrupting Attachments

Given the powerful psycho-emotional states provoked by historic urban places, it is unsurprising that changes to the familiar environment can disrupt attachments between people and place and cause the obverse: ontological insecurity. Loss of the familiar environment can produce both grief and dislocation which in turn can disrupt or even sever existing attachments as well as prevent the creation of new attachments between people and place.

This sense of loss, pain, and dislocation is particularly acute in times of rapid urban change such as with urban renewal initiatives in the 1960s and 1970s. For example, Fried showed how the loss of the familiar environment induced a process of grief not dissimilar to losing a loved one (2000) whereas Lynch (1960: 42) found an almost 'pathological attachment' to the remaining built environment during the urban renewal initiatives in North America and Fullilove (2016) identified the 'root shock' caused by forced displacement. Although not theorised as ontological insecurity, it is clear that within SAVE's early publications there was a deep awareness of the link between conservation and psycho-emotional states. For example, SAVE identified the 'stability signified by unchanging buildings', which they saw as 'psychologically valuable, particularly in a violent and rapidly changing world' (SAVE Britain's Heritage, 1975: 1289). It followed through with their understandings of the psychological impacts of urban change by again drawing attention to the psycho-emotional elements of conservation

> Underlying this article is the conviction that building conservation is of more than just practical importance. It is essential to the health and humanity of a community environment. Just as is common during times of war, massive destruction of a community's physical fabric as part of a plan for redevelopment can remove much of what provides a stabilising influence of people's lives. Stability in the built environment is needed to instill confidence in the future, whereas constant destruction and rebuilding can tear at the very heart of the community. The dislocation and sense of loss can break down the pride and respect that ordinary citizens may have in their hometown. What they had identified as being their world ceases to be part of them. (Binney, 1979: 25)

Here, SAVE acknowledged the complex emotional register bound up within the stability of a familiar environment as physical destruction was married with psychological dislocation as a person's everyday rhythms and routines were disrupted and the familiar became unfamiliar. In these ways, changes to the external environment ensured that 'the continued existence of familiar surroundings may satisfy a psychological need, which even if irrational, is very real' as 'nothing gives more tangible assurance of stability than bricks and mortar' (Cantell in Hubbard, 1993: 363).

A sense of dislocation was evident in the ways in which local residents viewed some of the conservation work on their town's historic buildings. For example, in Selkirk, the work to conserve the clock tower was met with a discussion about the effects of weathering on the look and feel of the town. Logan believed that the new stone 'sticks out like a sore thumb' but that within five years 'it'll be back to what it should be'. Logan went further to recall

> a spell when they used to power-blast buildings and they became very new looking 'cause they basically took off the grime, didn't they? And I always still felt it needed a wee ... something that's really power blasted needed a couple of years to return to its normal self. It almost looked naked if you like initially.

Sharon on the other hand 'didn't mind the patchiness' as 'the fact that it is an old thing that is new and ... really looked after, is a really positive thing, rather than just looking a bit faded and needing a bit of a face wash. I think that's really positive, in fact. Yes, look, back to how it started!' Here the temporal aspect of familiarity gained importance as the residents discussed the process of weathering to ensure that the building could continue to match their lived and felt experiences of their town. This exchange also highlights a key aspect of the intensity of attachments and the extent to which people felt uncomfortable or dissatisfied with change as opposed to the type of change that would fundamentally rupture their attachment to place as seen with the urban renewal initiatives of the mid to late twentieth century. The example of weathering did not come with a consensus nor strong emotional responses but rather a sense of in-the-moment dislocation and discomfort that would recede over time.

The spectrum from feeling dissatisfied with or detached from place was evident through the visceral reactions to new and replacement buildings. This was clearly expressed throughout SAVE Britain's Heritage's reports in the 1980s, as post-war redevelopment was decried across England. In Manchester, there was an awareness of 'considerable public disenchantment with the products of this period, a dislike for the oppressive architecture it produced, and a nostalgic interest in what was destroyed' (Powell, 1982b: np). This set of complex emotional responses fed into a general belief that the people of Manchester 'are dissatisfied with blank, bland and monotonous modern buildings' (Powell, 1982b: np). Gateshead was deemed to be a 'pleasureless, utilitarian place' and it was felt to be 'doubtful if future generations will find pleasure in the creations of post-war architects and planners there' (Powell, 1982c: np), whereas 'Wilfred Burn's 1967 prospectus for the rebuilding of Newcastle is a vision of horror' (Powell, 1982a: np). In Leeds, the emotional response was cooler than in Newcastle as 'the architectural form of the new development was profoundly disappointing', whereas other developments were seen to be 'uninspiring' (Powell, 1986: np). Here we can see the use of words such as 'disenchantment', 'dislike', 'dissatisfied', and 'disappointing', which suggests a lack of attachment to the new environment. However, it is important to note that attitudes and attachments can change over time as SAVE recognised that their 'own views on some of the buildings it originally campaigned against – such as the Gateshead car park – have been reversed' (Wilkinson, 2006: 109). Changes to the existing urban environment have the capacity to disrupt attachments between people and place. At times these can be temporary, as shown with the clock tower, whereas others can have a longer-lasting effect on both the place and on a person. This does not just arise from the demolition of existing buildings but also from the extent to which people can create new attachments with replacement buildings.

Intensity of Attachment to Place

Attachments to place can vary in their intensity and fluctuate both between people and over time. Sometimes there are strong attachments to place which are often demonstrated by a desire to exhibit place protective behaviour. One example of this is seen with SAVE Britain's Heritage work to both prevent the loss of historic buildings and put forward alternative schemes. Further examples can be seen with the use of community asset transfers, right to buy, and the use of community shares and participatory budgeting. At a local level, the decision by the Campbeltown-based South Kintyre Development Trust 'to acquire the building on behalf of the local community and to seek the necessary funding to redevelop the building and bring it back into full public use'[12] demonstrated the importance of this historic building to the people of Campbeltown:

> It's like the town hall. A group of people set out to achieve something and there are disasters and difficulties along the way, but they keep going and they get there in the end. There's real commitment to these buildings. And that's admirable. (Penny)

Action to prevent the loss and/or secure the future of a historic building could be seen solely in pragmatic terms yet a large body of evidence from environmental psychology suggests that this form of place protective behaviour is motivated by an attachment to place as shown by the local residents' strength of feelings towards their 'precious' Town Hall to which they felt a 'commitment' (Penny).

---

[12] https://www.townhallcampbeltown.com/history/

However, not all people develop attachments to all historic urban places. In Scottish towns, the emoji workshops saw residents vote 'neutral' when asked how particular historic urban places made them feel. Neutral was largely equivocated with indifference with residents in Campbeltown, Rothesay, and Paisley each stating they 'didn't care' about certain places which included museums, residential, and retail buildings. For example, in Paisley, the Secret Collection – a collection of museum items that were previously in storage drew a neutral response

Amanda: I put neutral 'cause yes, the history is important but paint on canvas . . . it's a record of a time or a place by a person, but nowadays, because they have an intrinsic value of pounds and whatever number of noughts comes after it, it gets skewed. 'cause look at the money that gets put into . . . they'll need to have insurance, they'll need to have special fire protections and environmental protections because as you say, folk coming in and . . . all of that. So all of that is money that's not being spent on people. It's being spent on squares of canvas with paint on it.

. . .

Joan: I'm neutral 'cause a lot of these paintings were stored away in the museum and they didnae find them until they had to move things.
Various: Aye.
Joan: So if they were that important, they should have been out in the museum –
Eleanor: Years ago.
Joan: Changed about. That's what I'm neutral.

Staying in Paisley, reasons for neutral responses could be summed up by a dialogue between the participants

Kirstin: You cannae make up your mind.
Vera: You dinnae care about it.
Various: Aye.
Vera: You didnae care one way or another if it's there or no there.

These neutral responses demonstrate that there can be either weak attachments to places or an absence of attachment. The origins of the place attachment field prioritised positive attachments to place and as such there remains a gap in the depth of understanding concerning weaker attachments and how people go through a process of detachment. Some of these aspects are explored through what Manzo (2014) has termed the 'shadow side' of place attachment, which sees home as both a safe and unsafe haven and through territorial conflicts (de Bakker, 2022). However, in the case of the emoji workshops in Campbeltown, Kirriemuir, Paisley, Rothesay, and Selkirk, the reasons related to the fact that residents felt no connection with the stories behind the buildings or the buildings had not formed part of their everyday experiences, or it didn't appear to fit with their narrative of place. Other reasons included having no memory of the place and/or feeling that they could not create future memories with the place due to the expense of visiting or the fact that the new use was not considered to be in line with the needs of existing residents.

Differing intensities of attachment to the same places were evident during the initial stages of the transition from deindustrial to post-industrial in the late twentieth century and were revealed through the conflicting positions adopted by different people. These positions were broadly based on the strong attachments of those for whom the towns were their home, their former workplace, and the site of numerous inter-generational stories, and the weaker attachments expressed by those charged with trying to secure a post-industrial future for the place. SAVE's reports outlined this tension:

> Housing reform, civic modernity, and economic revitalisation are being steered by a desire to get rid of the image of the Industrial Revolution. The mills and the chimneys, once the principal source of civic pride, are now looked upon by civic leaders with embarrassment, an embarrassment founded upon the belief that economic prosperity can only be achieved by erasing all that remains of the 19th century mill town. (Binney, 1979: 9)

In this example, we can see how competing priorities impinged on the heritage of Yorkshire towns which affected both the architectural and historic value of industrial heritage and attachments between people and their place. SAVE further demonstrated their awareness of these relationships between people and place through a comparative exploration of how people felt about and remembered their places in both Yorkshire and in the United States of America

> It may be true, as W.R. Mitchell says in his fascinating *Lancashire Mill Town Traditions* (1977), that 'the minds of veterans I met tended to filter out the grimmest memories retaining those that were counted attractive, not least the rich community life of the towns and local patriotism engendered by mill, street and place of worship'. (Binney, 1979: 3–4)

These memories were not just held internally or expressed through oral histories but also gradually translated into action to conserve the place's industrial heritage. This shift was seen in Halifax:

> Ten years ago, conservationists in Halifax were few and their cause, however worthy, seemed largely irrelevant to the future needs of a town dependent on its living on industry and commerce .... By the mid 1970s, however, concern about the destruction of Halifax's historic buildings was beginning to be expressed by local people and by distinguished outsiders. (Powell, 1983: np)

At the heart of these statements is a gradual realisation of why place matters and a desire to maintain a connection to what the place once was as it transitioned into an unknown future. However, these strong attachments to place were not often recognised by those for whom there was a stronger attachment to what the place could become and a desire to resolve a more pressing set of socio-economic priorities

> The need for conservation in Gateshead is often questioned. There are those who believe that nothing survives that is worth conserving, and moreover that conservation is irrelevant to the needs of the town – for good housing, more jobs and increased prosperity. (Powell, 1982c: np)

Heritage in this interpretation was seen by some as an irrelevance and a hindrance to plans to secure a prosperous future for the town. In both examples, a complex process of detachment and attachment plays out through different temporal horizons. For some, nurturing existing attachments is pre-eminent, for others a process of detachment happens as people become physically displaced and psychologically dislocated and people seek to form new attachments, whereas for others there is an attachment to an imagined future place. In each of these scenarios the feelings can be equally intense but can compete with one another. For example, an imagined and hoped-for attachment to a newly regenerated place can obscure powerful existing attachments to place yet these temporal horizons do not have to be in competition with one another. As SAVE recognised, 'for new buildings to be successful they must become part of a stable environment, with the city preserving its identity and sense of durability and permanence amid the changes' (Binney, 1979: 24). Through this lens, existing attachments could be nurtured, new ones built, and imagined futures realised. However, to achieve this 'planning must treat the existing environment with respect and care, and even with love, rather than inflicting conventional formulae on to unique situations' (Binney, 1979: 25). Within this context, it is difficult to see how a 'one size fits all' approach could be taken as the intensity of attachments will vary in each time and each place and between people. Of crucial importance here is ensuring that both existing and future attachments to place are validated within the process of urban change.

Conclusion

This section has demonstrated that historic urban places matter emotionally because they have the capacity to stimulate and disrupt emotional attachments between people and place. The emotional attachments outlined in this section arose from two key themes. Firstly, attachments are existentially connected to a psycho-emotional state of ontological (in)security and secondly, they are derived from our everyday lived and felt experiences of familiar urban places. The type, nature, extent, and pace of urban change fundamentally shapes the ways in which people form attachments, the extent to which these attachments are disrupted, and the intensity of peoples' attachment to historic urban places.

The temporal dimension of historic place attachment assumes a key role within this analysis. The permanence and stability of a familiar environment ensures that there is potential for more people to develop rhythms, routines, stories, memories, and meanings that translate into emotional responses and emotional attachments. Furthermore, emotional attachments to historic urban places are formed, disrupted, and vary in their intensities because the past, present and future co-exist in both the psycho-emotional and everyday emotional register. In this interpretation, the past does not de facto assume precedence in the formation and maintenance of emotional attachments. Rather, it is a fusion of the recalled, felt, and imagined experiences of historic urban places – of what they were, are, and could become – that informs attachment. Crucial within this is therefore the recognition that emotional attachments are fluid and are not fixed in time, in person, or in place – attachments can form, strengthen, evolve, and weaken and can differ between people in the same place. As such, as this section has highlighted, emotional attachments are not universal, and people can have strong or weak attachments and/or become detached from historic urban places. The examples in this section build from emotional responses to demonstrate the complex processes through which emotional attachments are formed and disrupted and the varying intensities of these attachments to historic urban places. The extent to which these are individually formed or communally shared is the subject of the next section, as we move to consider the third aspect of the conceptual framework: emotional communities.

4 Emotional Communities

The term 'community' is notoriously difficult and contested but can be defined, in a legal context, as a 'common interest, identity or geography' (Community Empowerment Act (Scotland) 2015: 2). This section extends this definition by introducing emotion more explicitly into our understanding of community. In so doing, the section is located within work that seeks to move our understandings of communities towards the 'emotional' (Rosenwein, 2006), 'feeling' (Pernau, 2017), and 'affective' (Zink, 2019). In particular the section extends Barbara Rosenwein's (2006) work on 'emotional communities', defined as 'groups in which people adhere to the same norms of emotional expression and value – or devalue – the same or related emotions' by focusing on emotional responses and attachments (2). The Element therefore defines emotional communities as 'collectives who hold and value – or devalue – a shared set of emotional responses and attachments to historic urban places'. This definition can work with heritage practice by putting it into conversation with the definition of 'heritage community' from the *Convention on the Value of Cultural Heritage for Society* (*Faro Convention*), which 'consists of people who value specific aspects of cultural heritage which they wish, within the framework of public action, to sustain and transmit to future generations' (Council of Europe, 2005: Article 2b). Within this framing it is the 'individual's emotional attachment' to cultural heritage that determines their 'participation in a particular community' (Swedish National Heritage Board, 2014). This section brings these two understandings together to consider two types of emotional communities: place-based and practice-based.

Place-Based Emotional Communities

As Sections 2 and 3 showed, a person's emotional relationship with historic places develops from their lived and felt experiences. These place-based experiences ingrain meanings and memories resulting from our everyday rhythms and routines. Being in place, thinking about place, and using place are each key components of how and why we respond emotionally and form attachments. Each of these experiences can be intensely individual but they cannot be divorced from their shared social context, as such historic places have the capacity to produce emotional communities who can value and share a similar emotional register.

In Campbeltown, the emoji workshop revealed that residents either felt very happy and happy when asked how the Picture House made them feel (Figure 5). The reasons for this shared response were at once individual and communal

> I think as well it's the only cinema, I know there was the Rex years and years ago when I was about . . . <laughs> It's the only one so all of us have probably gone to it and every child has gone to it at some point, so you'll have a memory of being in that cinema and at different things, whereas if you were maybe in a city you could go to a cinema, . . . cinema, an East End, West End, so everyone's got some sort of memory attached to that scary film, happy film, school trips – and I think that's probably a big thing with it as well. And I love the Romeo and Juliet balconies in there! (Sally).

Here, Sally reflects the interplay of individual and collective experiences. In essence Sally tells us how our individual experiences can be mediated through collective experiences in public and shared spaces. Together these experiences are both deeply personal and widely shared. The result is a cumulative layering of

Figure 5 Campbeltown Picture House
Source: Canmore, Historic Environment Scotland: DP 142574 © Crown Copyright: HES. All Rights' Reserved.

individual and collective memories resulting from shared experiences in public spaces which gives rise, in this case, to a set of conventionally positive emotions. However, place-based emotional communities do not just share positive emotional responses. This was most evident within a wider discussion of Campbeltown, as both pride and shame co-existed and manifested in individual place-protective behaviour through a sense of feeling defensive about their town

Isla: And unfortunately, the town had scaffolding all round it at the same time, didn't it? Two years ago the whole town was just . . . and it was good because it was progression, there was stuff happening, but everything was so ugly and depressing and you'd get these people posting stuff on Facebook: 'I was down in Campbeltown, and it was looking terrible.' I went, 'Yeah, 'cause we've just invested £10 million in the area!' But all they could see is the . . . and you feel very . . .

Lee: Defensive.

Isla: Defensive, that's exactly the word! Do you know, I feel really defensive about anything that anybody says about the place!

. . ..

Isla: My kids are like that as well, and even though they're younger, they're very much like that as well. They go mad about any of these negative comments and stuff. It really annoys me.

At the root of this exchange that evoked conventionally negative responses, however, was a deep sense of attachment to Campbeltown as demonstrated by the residents subsequent actions on social media. Here, residents discussed how they responded passionately to any negative comments made about the town in a very public defence of place. In so doing, place-based emotional communities contested the different images of the town through a virtual medium that in turn served to reinforce and strengthen attachments to physical places. These feelings also moved from the individual to the collective in terms of contesting comments made on social media. This example also illustrates that there is not just one place-based emotional community, and there can also be conflict between place-based emotional communities. However, identifying which communities exist, what their shared values and emotions are, and how they may be in conflict with one another, provides a better sense of the kinds of emotional responses and attachments that exist in place.

Emotional communities, in Rosenwein's definition, share and value similar emotions. However, this is often mediated and realised through collective discussion. For example, the process of sharing how people felt about historic places within an emoji workshop in Rothesay saw instinctive individual responses change as each participant listened to and reflected on the collective discussion. Heather, for example, changed from very happy to neutral based on shifting from her memories of what Rothesay Pavilion (Figure 6) enabled the community to do including attending concerts, playing five-a-side, debating issues within the Community Council, and going to dances to a focus on what the re-opened Pavilion might prevent, hinder, or exclude the existing community from doing. This point was discussed further as the group then turned to consider examples where the retrofit of other buildings across the UK was perceived to have 'separated the community from the building' (Cameron). As the discussion continued, Heather again shifted – 'Yeah, it's starting to make me angry actually' – and other participants also started to both change and blend their immediate responses in the light of the group discussion:

Catriona: I went for happy because I think there is the medium between both the it'll be great, it's exciting and the concerns and so I suppose on balance I'm optimistic and I'm hopeful that it will be everything everybody wants it to be, but I'm just also slightly wary and cautious and we'll see what happens.

. . .

Catriona: This would probably move from sad to excited, a bit . . .
Cameron: Yeah, nervous <chuckles>.
Catriona: . . . nervous yeah, yeah.

Figure 6 Rothesay Pavilion

Source: Canmore, Historic Environment Scotland: SC 977802 © Crown Copyright: HES. All Rights' Reserved.

These kinds of emotional responses are common among place-based emotional communities when their use of 'their' places comes under threat (Madgin et al., 2018). Responses were heightened through collective discussion, whether in person or through social media, as increased knowledge of other people's perceptions and lived and felt experiences shape and inform people's ongoing emotional relationships with place. However, solely focusing on the expression of emotional responses does not fully reveal the reasons why people coalesce into emotional communities. Here, it is crucial to go deeper to ascertain what people are attached to and how this is shaping their responses. For example, in Rothesay there was an attachment to the activities that the Pavilion enabled, whereas in Kirriemuir, a strong attachment to the materiality of the 'wee red toun' was in evidence

Molly: It's what it could be that makes you angry when you look at it, you think oh my goodness, if this was just done up like the rest of the town's been done up, it would be a beautiful building. I mean I go on about the stones but really, I mean they're so unique in Kirrie, that stone is just lovely. It really is, isn't it? I trail my hands along it every time I pass and think how long has this been here, you know?

...

Ava: If you see Kirriemuir in a late autumn evening with the sun shining on the red sandstone, it comes alive. It absolutely comes alive!

Molly: Beautiful as you go up the Roods, beautiful.

Ava: It's amazing, especially with an autumn sun on it. It's just spectacular. It's wonderful.

Joseph: Came from a local quarry.

Ava: Absolutely beautiful.

Holly: Which no longer exists, so it's not replaceable.

...

Ava: I mean it is porous, I know there are difficulties with it, 'cause it is porous, the sandstone here.

...

Ava: And you can see that after a rainstorm, you see all the sandstone dust lying on the pavements and everything, so to be absolutely objective I suppose there are slight difficulties with it, yeah, but it is ... the way it looks, I think it looks great.

Molly: If you just go round Kirrie and look at the stones ... you'll know what we're talking about. Just do it, and then you'll know why Kirrie is so special.

In Kirriemuir (Figure 7), it is clear that these residents both value and have a shared attachment to the materiality of place. Any attempt to change or deviate from the use of red sandstone would make people angry, likely because their attachment to place would be disrupted. Anger, in this instance, masquerades as a negative emotion, but through the lens of attachment we can see that the response needs to be contextualised and actually reflects a positive set of feelings towards place. Without such a positive attachment to place it is doubtful if anger could be expressed. Looking beyond the response and towards the attachment therefore gives a deeper understanding of why people coalesce into emotional communities.

Together, the Picture House, Campbeltown, the Rothesay Pavilion, and the 'wee red toun' demonstrate how individual and collective lived and felt experiences of public spaces can produce rich emotional responses that cannot just be taken at face value as they are often underpinned by deeply held attachments. Running alongside this is the architectural and historic value of the buildings and their materiality. In each example, the way the Picture House, Campbeltown, the Rothesay Pavilion and Kirriemuir looked in terms of their architecture, materiality, and/or present-day condition were referenced by residents as to why these places mattered emotionally to them. This valorisation of the built fabric could not, however, be divorced from their daily rhythms and routines and their ingrained memories resulting from their lived and felt experiences of place. Place-based emotional communities are therefore relational and informed by the relationships between social experiences and the physical look and feel of historic places.

Figure 7 Kirriemuir 31 High Street, Town House
Source: Canmore, Historic Environment Scotland: SC 2625533 © Crown Copyright: HES. All Rights' Reserved.

Practice-Based Emotional Communities

The Authorised Heritage Discourse (AHD) developed by Laurajane Smith (2020) highlights the 'emotional neutrality' (53) of heritage decision-making. This is supported by work within the wider built environment sector, which suggests that 'planners typically conceptualise themselves as professionals not emotionally engaged with their work' (Ferriera, 2013: 703). Evidence to support the AHD/rational planning system was particularly apparent as some built environment professionals shared a view that emotion is synonymous with subjectivity. In this view, emotion was seen as the antonym of rational and objective decision-making and therefore should be rejected within professionalised decision-making including designation and managing change. In the context of heritage designation, built environment professional Howard supported Smith's work on the AHD as he discussed the need for criteria and therefore how the process is 'not particularly emotional'. Howard also supported Hoch's findings with regards to the planning system:

> You have to be dispassionate in a way, you can't ... because being too emotional has little place in the planning system. You have to have specific reasons, if you wanna object for something, you have to have absolute concrete justification for objection. You can't just say, 'Well, this such a nice building', <laughs> it's much more scientific than that. And you have to look at the law in detail and policies, you have to understand how they work.

A further built environment professional, Joe, supported Howard's views, stating, 'I'm not a great fan of emotional reactions, either one way or the other. There's no emotion involved to what I'm saying. I'm saying this is going to have to be removed because ... I'm not emotionally involved in that decision. It's a practical thing.' Joe went further to talk through how his 'love' of historic buildings had to be factored out within his own professional decision-making processes

> I love historic architecture and I love good buildings, but there's almost a professional veneer that goes over the whole thing that says, 'Well beyond thinking about how lovely this is, I've moved into the state of how do we deal with this, how do we make this work? So it probably quite quickly moves on from my own personal feelings towards the buildings that are involved. I think professionally I'm completely aware of the broad and objective value of the historic environment and all the individual buildings, and it very quickly moves on from that.

Why Historic Places Matter Emotionally 47

Across these examples we can see that certain words signal practices that align with the lexicon attached to AHD/rational planning system: 'dispassionate', 'concrete', 'scientific', 'practical', and 'objective'. When asked separately if emotion was considered within decision-making built environment professionals, Howard and Martin, both gave similar answers by stating that we are 'absolutely objective' (Howard) and 'completely objective' (Martin). However, over the course of the answer, Martin shifted to consider the boundaries between personal and professional but rested with a belief that emotion, both as a way of decision-making and category of information, was at best a tiny aspect of decision-making

> Interesting question ... when you started the question, I was no, no, it's all completely objective ... and a lot of it is, quite frankly ... But there is some emotion in it I guess, and sometimes you look at a building and you just say well that's a really nice building. I got involved in working in the built environment 'cause I like the built ... it's something I've got a passion about, and I'm interested in architecture, and I'm interested in all of those sorts of things, so yeah, but would that emotional attachment influence the decisions? ... Are those decisions influenced by some kind of emotional attachment? <Sighs> At the margins possibly.

To go from this position to suggest that heritage and wider built environment professionals could coalesce into a community that values emotion therefore feels quite a leap. However, there are two caveats here. First, while it is clear that some built environment professionals favour objectivity and apply a detached and rational approach to considering heritage designation and planning applications, this does not rule out the existence of emotion. Here, we can explore the extent to which 'neutrality and rationality, or affecting a "cool logic", are all states of emotional being' (Smith, 2020: 49). Smith, in the context of emotions within museums/heritage sites, develops the discussion to state that 'the flat emotions of professional practice, where an "objective emotional neutrality" may be striven for, are nonetheless as much as an affective practice as public memorialising and commemorating the grief and distress of historical atrocities' (61). If we apply this logic in the context of Rosenwein's definition then a practice-based emotional community is evident in the ways in which built environment professionals collectively value a flatter emotional register within their decision-making processes.

Second, it is also apparent that some built environment professionals did demonstrate shared emotional responses and attachments to historic urban places. This was most evident at a personal level, where a number of built environment professionals expressed positive emotional responses to historic urban places. For example, Martin, like Joe, talked of his 'love' of history and the historic environment:

> And then trying to divorce the business perspective from the personal perspective becomes quite difficult, and I guess from my own individual, personal perspective, as somebody fascinated by history, I love history, I read a lot of history, then it is the history actually, the thinking about what happened in those buildings, or why those buildings were built or what was going on around those buildings, and trying to imagine a past which is what a lot of history is about; it's just trying to imagine what it felt like and what it was like to be in that place at that time. The buildings can give you some very strong clues to that. So it gives you a different view on history and on the world.

This was supported by the fact that Roy felt

> Passionate about history. It is my favourite subject. My leisure time is spent reading. If I had a choice of a book to read on a long flight or a long train journey, I would always go for a history book. It is the association with the past, it is the interest of the fact that buildings have been witness to generations of people.

This interest in the past, in imagining what it felt like to live in or use the buildings in the past, was further developed both by Martin, who recalled visiting historic sites, and Lesley who reflected on walking through a mix of old and new buildings:

> I won't be particularly fascinated, going round a historic house or something, I won't be thinking about the beautiful drapes or beautiful all of that, or the paintings are all beautiful or whatever; I'd be probably more interested in the kitchen and all the stuff in the kitchen and thinking about how did the people live who were working in that kitchen. So it's a way of reimagining history, I guess. (Martin)

> And this is my point about the fascination of walking around London that you can walk past modern buildings, you turn the corner and there's this curious church, you turn another corner there's a tower. I think it's amazing. (Lesley)

'Love', 'passion', 'fascination', 'amazement', 'interest', and 'imagination' are each words that reoccurred in the shared emotional register of built environment professionals when considering their own emotional relationships with historic urban places. In addition, built environment professionals also expressed their attachments to historic urban places as well. For example, Roy reflected on his own family history in which buildings in his childhood city had repeatedly been demolished to state that 'buildings matter to me because of the importance that they have in tying today's community back into history'. Here Roy's familial lived experience gave him a deeply felt awareness of the importance of historic buildings. This sense of attachment to historic place was also demonstrated by a number of built environment professionals, exemplified by Mark who reflected many of the themes outlined in Section 3 by talking about an awareness of the need for identity, safety, and security and how the historic environment can act as an anchor

> I talked earlier about how the existing built environment anchors us. I think we all need to feel secure in our lives and the built environment is part of that feeling of security. You need to know that when you leave your house it is going to look like it did yesterday. That is the past. There is a feeling of security and anchoring.

Among built environment professionals there is therefore evidence of a group of people that 'adhere to the same norms of emotional expression and value–or devalue–the same or related emotions' (Rosenwein, 2006: 2) whether that is in embracing a 'cool logic' or by demonstrating a positive emotional relationship with the past. The extent to which this is replicated within professional organisations is less clear. Using the example of SAVE in their early years, between 1975 and 1991, it is evident that there is an awareness of the emotional relationships held by place-based communities in much of their work. SAVE outlined, 'The root of our belief is that people do care about the places where they live, work and shop, that they are concerned about the devastation meted out to historic towns since the Second World War' (Binney and Watson Smyth, 1991: 22). This rhetoric was matched by the reality that SAVE often collaborated with place-based organisations as part of their campaign work. Indeed, as with pairing with the Derby Civic Society (Figure 8), much of SAVE's work took 'the form of Mayday calls from local people concerned about the imminent loss of a local landmark' (11) and through this delicate balance of national amenity society and local issue were able to demonstrate an awareness of the psycho-emotional consequences of urban change.

For example, in Manchester, SAVE recognised that the demolition of the Lancaster Arcade was: '(as the Victorian Society commented), "a subject highly emotive to many Mancunians"' (Powell, 1982b: np). SAVE went further to match emotion to action by suggesting, 'The old heart of Manchester needs new life and new prosperity. Its people are dissatisfied with blank, bland and monotonous modern buildings. Manchester cannot afford to consign the Cathedral Conservation Area to the bulldozer' (Powell, 1982b: np). In this example, there was therefore an awareness both of the fact that there was an emotional relationship between Mancunians and Manchester and that retaining historic buildings was an

Figure 8 Cutting the Heart out of Derby: Report by SAVE Britain's Heritage
Source: Copyright SAVE Britain's Heritage. Image drawn by Robin Ollington. All Rights' Reserved.

essential part of preserving this relationship. Contained within this is the capability within the organisation to ascertain the emotional register of place-based communities. This was not just restricted to Manchester. SAVE's original manifesto spoke of the 'pain' of loss in general (SAVE Britain's Heritage, 1975: 1289), and a report into Liverpool recognised that 'more than perhaps any other major British city, it inspires affection amongst its natives and a deep fascination amongst outsiders' (Powell, 1982a: np). In Leeds, SAVE felt, 'The clearances were motivated by idealistic intentions, but the results were not entirely happy. Ancient communities were ruthlessly scattered and the new housing estates were even bleaker that those of the 1930s' (Powell, 1986, np). However, in Newcastle, 'The town centre has been largely wrecked and it is doubtful if future generations will find pleasure in the creations of post-war architects and planners there' (Powell, 1982c: np).

The work of an organisation to prevent the loss of historic places is a highly emotive practice and SAVE crucially took the form of finding 'sympathetic developers and investors in the commercial sector' and supporting numerous alternative schemes to come forward (Binney, 2016: 3–6). Marcus Binney (2016), now Executive President of SAVE, recalled, 'Above all, over these forty years, ours has been a message of hope: that great buildings can live again, giving satisfaction, delight and inspiration to all who see and use them' (13). This message of hope was transformed into sustained action by SAVE by bringing together and working with other built environment professionals and place-based communities to recognise the past, present, and future values of historic places. In so doing, SAVE repeatedly demonstrated an acute awareness of the role of emotion within the process of conservation and could therefore be said to 'adhere to the same norms of emotional expression and value–or devalue–a shared set' (Rosenwein, 2006:2) of emotional responses and attachments to historic urban places

Conclusion

This section has demonstrated that historic urban places matter emotionally because communities develop shared emotional registers. Both place- and practice-based emotional communities coalesce around a shared set of emotional responses and demonstrate collective attachments to historic urban places. This is evident both by the words used by local residents and built environment professionals and their actions including investing in and working with historic urban places, campaigning for historic urban places, and commenting on social media feeds. We can also identify examples within both place- and practice-based emotional communities where these responses and attachments and the very notion of emotion are contested. Emotional communities, like any community, are not homogenous and are conditioned by a range of different factors including positionality, power, and professionalised contexts. However, at root we can identify that emotional communities exist and at times they overlap and at times they are in tension. The next section turns to consider the ways in and extent to which the heritage and planning system can productively recognise and work with the responses and attachments of emotional communities.

5 Recognising Emotion

> Emotional attachments to historic urban places are 'implicit as opposed to explicit ... I don't think it's necessarily talked about. But I think people recognise the importance of it.' (Cassie)

> There is a gap there between emotion and the planning system, but I would say that is because the system is not recognising it. (Mark)

The ability to work productively with emotion in the form of responses, attachments, and communities is conditioned by the extent to which it can be recognised within existing systems. Built environment professionals, Cassie and Mark, demonstrated the complicated ways in which emotion is recognised within existing systems. This section develops the findings from Sections 2, 3, and 4 to see the ways in and extent to which emotional responses, attachments and communities are recognised within place-based decision-making. This is achieved by exploring how emotion, as a category of information, can be used to shape the type, nature, and extent of urban change. In so doing, the section moves from a discussion of individuals and place/practice-based communities towards focusing on the systems and structures within which people's emotional responses and attachments can be expressed and recognised. This work is located in a growing area of scholarship that examines the role of emotion within decision-making including place-marketing (Lecompte et al., 2017), urban cultural policy (Borén et al., 2021), and real estate and property development (Fallon, 2022). Common across these place-based issues is a desire to see emotion as a valid way of making decisions and therefore disrupt the traditional argument within some, mainly Western branches of philosophy led by Descartes and Stoicism, which favour a split between reason and emotion and thus a depriviliging of emotion. In so doing, the section critically examines the notion that emotion cannot be trusted and/or that it distorts place-based decision-making.

From Words to Action

As seen in Section 1, there has been considerable evolution in the rhetoric that surrounds both the heritage and planning systems in the UK. This rhetorical shift is reflective of a more fundamental challenge to the traditional view of the inherent value of heritage as being rooted in physical fabric only to be uncovered by professional experts (the Authorised Heritage Discourse) by a more people-centred approach that instead pluralises both what can be seen as heritage and who can ascribe value. Much of the impetus for this move is expressed through international heritage charters, which outline evolving approaches to determining cultural significance and managing change in the historic environment, such as the revised *Burra Charter* (1999), the *Faro Convention* (2005), the *Quebec Declaration* (2008), and most recently the *People-Centred Resolution* from the International Council of Monuments and Sites (ICOMOS), which resolved to:

> Promote people-centered approaches, the connections of people with heritage and places; intercultural dialogue and understanding, sustainability and well-being when addressing local, national, and international heritage policies and practice (December 2020).

The extent to which this rhetorical shift is matched by changes to policies and practices is more limited. However, built environment professionals did reflect on three areas where policy and practice had developed in the twenty-first century in ways that could, in theory, recognise emotion. The first one was in England, through the introduction of communal values within Historic England's *Conservation Principles,* which are intended to help guide and manage change in the historic environment. Both the original principles (2008) and the Consultation Document on the Conservation Principles (2017) contain explicit references to emotion. In terms of how this could move beyond rhetoric, built environment professional Mark discussed the following:

> In general terms, communal value is something that I can see being difficult for a developer because it is bringing the emotion in and giving that a recognition in a way that is harder to challenge, partly because it is unexpected and difficult to pin down. I think the way you bring it in is through significance. If part of what makes a building significant is people's emotional attachment to that building, then that is something that will be recognised and I think is recognised.

A second way in which people's attachments to place could be recognised was expressed by built environment professional Roy who stated, 'The public sector equality duty is an area where judges have to grapple with the question of whether a decision was taken having regard to the due interests of communities.' While Roy went on to recognise that it is the

> sort of area where the law does have to take account of strength of feeling and pride and the right to have your voice heard ... you would rarely find a case that was deflected by an acceptance that pride mattered, but what you do get is judges saying things like, 'There are strongly, keenly held views about this matter and I must have regard to the strength of feeling.'

Here, emotion and feeling were recognised within existing legal processes, even if as Roy further stated this was 'mostly about the need to comply with the right to be heard'.

A third way in which the changing regulatory environment has opened up the potential for attachment to be recognised within the system comes through community ownership in both England and Scotland. Here, Roy talked of the link between assets of community value (ACV) and how people's attachments to place reveal their sense of felt ownership:

> We see the ACV process in use all the time. Pubs, commonly. That is another aspect of where people feel they own something . . . . The pub is challenged by dwindling community support, but people have a lot of strong association with the place because the pub for them was, and for many of them they wish it still was and perhaps it still is, a point in the community which is a meeting place for people. It is a socialising thing for different facets of the community . . . . They were trying to get something protected a, an ACV. It is a convergence of totally different philosophies that feel the concrete, tangible things – buildings – are part of the physical manifestation of their heritage.

As recognised in Section 3, pubs have the capacity to be an anchor in a changing urban world, which in turn can motivate the type of place protective behaviour mentioned by Roy. In Scotland, this was paralleled by the case of Campbeltown Town Hall and the Picture House, which are both owned on behalf of the local community and, like pubs, shows that there is an outlet for people's attachment to place to be recognised in law.

Running alongside these policy/practice developments are also a raft of financial mechanisms that now enable attachments to place recognised through direct action. For example, the use of community shares, participatory budgeting, and grant schemes from organisations like the National Lottery Heritage Fund each offer a way in which communities felt ownership can transfer into legal ownership (Madgin in Kintrea and Madgin, 2019). However, there must be a note of caution within these financial mechanisms, as they each put the onus on emotional communities being able to buy, redevelop, and maintain historic places. The extent to which attachments to place can be nurtured is therefore conditioned by economic and logistical factors. Systems that enable the everyday experiences of place to transition from felt ownership into actual ownership may be nascent, but the lens of emotion helps to develop a fuller understanding of how and why these mechanisms are taken up by place-based communities.

Locating Emotion

The rest of this section moves away from the macro policy level to instead focus on a place-based analysis. Within this, it is possible to identify six broad areas from the research in which emotion, in the form of responses, attachments, and communities, was recognised within decisions about individual sites (Figure 9).

Why Historic Places Matter Emotionally 55

Figure 9 Where emotion is located within urban development

Source: We Are Cognitive (Madgin, 2021c). All Rights' Reserved. The above infographic can be split into two key themes: working with existing emotional relationships and negotiating new emotional relationships and forms the basis of the following sections.

Existing Emotional Relationships

Debating change within historic urban places is arguably the most emotive aspect of heritage and planning. This can take place within both written and verbal settings, and it can also take place within planning offices, courtrooms, place-based campaigns, and community engagement initiatives. In the context of planning objections, built environment professional Mark stated that the 'decision maker – the planning inspector or the secretary of state – can't put a lot of weight on how passionately you believe something in the majority of cases'. Emotion can be expressed and recognised but on its own it is unlikely to be persuasive

> I was at one inquiry many, many years ago which was going quite well until somebody who lived nearby presented an incredibly passionate piece of evidence on what it would mean for his daily life. It changed the course of that inquiry, but for me that is because he exposed some of the faults in the case rather than everyone felt sympathetic to his cause. (Mark)

Here, it is evident that emotion, as a way of making arguments or decisions, is contested within a highly professionalised context in which decisions about the future of places are carefully and judiciously considered alongside a range of other factors. However, if we look beyond emotion as a way of passionately presenting an argument, we can start to see that there are emotional categories of information within the argument. For example, built environment professional Roy, continuing the legal theme, recognised the following:

> Other cases I can see where you are at a public inquiry where emotions are running high I can fully understand because the people who are the professionals turning up to the inquiry, the decision makers, the inspector are here today, gone tomorrow. This is our community. They are playing around with our community. They are running out all these arguments, trotting out all this stuff, but they will be zooming off to the next one and we are left behind. We have to pay the price for this.

In both examples, we can see that emotional arguments are likely to be informed by a person's existing attachments to the place they are arguing for. The extent to which these attachments are neglected or rejected within the system was recognised by Paisley resident Thelma, who stated, 'Change of use happens without reference to the people who would use the facilities.' This statement opens up a conversation surrounding both the inclusion of local people in decision-making and also their everyday experiences of using places which can shape the ways in which attachments are formed and/or disrupted through existing systems.

In order to present passionately and infuse your language with anger, fear, joy, or pride, it is likely that a person holds a profound attachment to that place and is, as seen in Section 4, engaging in place-protective behaviour. In essence, the people and communities recognised by Mark and Roy are trying to convey what their place means to them in the ways that feel most authentic to them. This may not always be in the measured and detached rhetoric more common to legal processes but rather their form of expression is true to how place-based communities feel about their place and the future that they need for their sense of self and sense of place. Roy alluded to this through the use of 'our community' and how a sense of not understanding the needs and desires of place-based communities provoked raw emotions. An emotional argument therefore may not just be a rhetorical device but, as Roy partially demonstrated, through active and deep listening it is possible to hear the variety of responses and recognise the deep attachments held by place-based emotional communities. Here, it is important to note that the professionalised systems and structures that underpin both the heritage and planning systems in the UK have ingrained particular ways of communicating and validating particular forms of expert knowledge. In the two examples recalled by Mark and Roy, we can identify a clash in the preferred styles of communication (Ruiz et al., 2019). This is both verbal and written as Mark reflects 'the emotional side is very much at the forefront of what we do, even though it may not come across in the documents. It is hard to express that.' We can also see that the emotional information in the messages conveyed by local residents and communities cannot yet be validated within the existing systems. This does not mean, however, that emotional relationships do not exist but rather that, in these examples, they are not able to be fully recognised and therefore neglected or rejected as valid forms of information that can shape decisions concerning possible futures for historic urban places.

A fear that the attachments that people held for their places would not be validated was evident across the conversations with residents and took many different forms. In Kirriemuir, this was grounded in a belief that the red sandstone from the 'wee red toun' would be lost and any place protective action that could result from this.

Ava: It's a feature of Kirriemuir and I wouldn't like to see any of that taken away really. That's my opinion.

Holly: ... but the red sandstone there, it costs a lot to dress it so it's actually wind and water-tight and I know that 'cause it was roughcast before, the chances are whoever takes that building on will apply for planning permission and say it was roughcast before, and because it was roughcast before they will get permission and it will be roughcast again 'cause it's cheaper and easier to do, and it will not look like the nice wee red sandstone building that you're talking about.

Ava: Well, have to resist it then.

This desire to 'resist' in Kirriemuir was matched by campaigns led by SAVE, often in partnership with local organisations. For example, in Gateshead, SAVE reported how 'a spirited campaign was mounted by the many local people who did not want to leave their homes' (Powell, 1982c: np), whereas in the case of Yorkshire mills, SAVE drew on the published work of Tamara Haraven and

Randolph Langenbach in North America to demonstrate 'the factory workers and their families had a very special feeling for the massive industrial buildings all around them' (Binney, 1979: 3). *Satanic Mills,* the book of the exhibition held in 1979 'sold out within ten days' mainly to local people, who believed: 'These mills are part of our lives. We don't want them torn down' (SAVE, 2005: 18). In Newcastle, the emphasis was placed on businesses: 'The tenants shared the local press's fears that the arcade (Handyside Arcade, Percy Street) would be "Eldonised" and its character lost. They saw clearly the threat to their own livelihoods' (Powell, 1982a: np). Within each of these examples we can see that SAVE recognised that people have attachments to their homes, industrial buildings, and the character of retail areas. If we go further we can see that these attachments were based on both the use of the built environment and their historic and architectural interest. These are just a handful of examples where a national organisation was able to understand the needs and desires of place-based emotional communities formed of residents, civic organisations, and businesses in ways that could retain meaningful places for local communities and thus provide the opportunity for existing attachments to be nurtured rather than neglected.

In the context of working with the public, there were mixed views. In Paisley, some local residents were sceptical about 'consultation':

Amanda: There's no such thing as a consultation process.
Eleanor: Exactly!
Amanda: They've made up their mind what they want. They'll come and they'll ask a select number of people the questions and then they go and they rip it up and throw it in the bin, and you get what they wanted in the first place.
Eleanor: Quite agree with you.

This view is mirrored in the wider literature, and is perhaps best expressed by Grosvenor (2019), an international organisation involved in urban property, who found trust levels in development were low and could be restored if 'predicated on a better quality conversation between local councils, private developers and the public' (7). In addition to this, the Quality of Life Foundation, in conjunction with Landsec, found that 'trust is vital but often absent in community engagement processes' and that they 'need to listen to communities in a meaningful way', which 'may require more creative and interactive methods of community engagement, rather than just surveys and interviews' (Quality of Life Foundation and Landsec, 2023: 5). Despite an increasing focus on people-centred approaches, there remains a lack of trust in planning and development. Moves to improve practice are now evident through the Community Charter put forward by

Grosvenor (2020), and through an increasing focus on people-centred methods (Edwards and Purohit, 2023).

On the ground, this was shown by built environment professional Rachel who talked of the need to recognise existing emotional communities, particularly in the context of understanding their collective memories and seeing their historic places as *lieux de memoire* rather than a development site

> And as I said, it's often not about the new building, it's about the loss of something that's very difficult, you know very difficult to hold onto. But at the same time to draw the non-traditional campaign groups into a debate you have to work with emotion because if we wrote to them and said, 'We really want to talk about 40,000 square foot of commercial space and 200 units of . . . ' no one's interested in that . . . So you have to use emotion and memory and community sort of language to try and engage with people, otherwise they're gonna just say, 'I'm not interested.'

Rachel was attuned to the fact that emotion is an integral aspect of people's relationships with place and that the traditional communication styles ingrained within heritage and planning systems can often clash. While there may have been a clash of communication styles in legal settings described earlier by Mark and Roy, here Rachel actively worked with emotion as both information and method to understand place and the consequences of change. In a similar vein, Grace talked about having to work with the grain of place, to recognise that people held attachments to place names and the need to validate their desires and emotions, in this case pride, within any future plans

> In Sheffield there is a John Lewis, but it is called or was called Cole Brothers. All the older generation, even though they rebranded the shop, still called it Cole Brothers because that is what they knew. There are all these things that you can try and change, but you won't – not whilst there are people alive who can remember. You won't change that because to them it's Cole Brothers. Why would they call it anything else? I think it was that understanding that people were very proud of their city, and you didn't want to alienate them by presupposing that what they wanted.

Rachel and Grace aligned, in the language of this Element, with a need to identify existing place-based emotional communities: to understand how individuals and collectives felt about their places through using different types of community engagement exercises. Rachel and Grace both alluded to the importance of memory, whether as a result of living, visiting, or working with place, within the formation of responses, attachments, and communities. Rachel went one step further to state that, in her experience, often 'the attachment is around the memories, not about the building'. Rachel's view, however, can be taken further to consider the relationship between the memory and the building and in particular how memories of a place can give people a sense of felt ownership. This is a type of ownership that has no legal basis in that it does not refer to private property rights or government ownership. Instead, it is informed by psycho-emotional experiences in which people feel like their investment in place is so powerful that their attachment can manifest as felt ownership. In essence, their feelings are powerful due to the intensity of their emotional attachment to the historic place. This was eloquently explained by a built environment professional, Roy, as he discussed Covent Garden: 'Covent Garden is a greatly cherished and much-loved piece of the urban landscape. It is owned by the public really in a sense. Well, it is owned by Capital & Counties, but the public – and I would be one of them – feel that I have a stake in it'. Local resident Isla, in Section 2, also touched on this, believing that 'people have got ownership of the Picture House'. We can build on this to consider the ways in which memories embedded in place may be at risk of being lost between generations. In Burnley, SAVE discussed the intangible elements of conservation in which these intergenerational stories of place and the attachments that they generate may be lost as places undergo radical change

> Yet there are less tangible, if no less important arguments for conservation. The eminent Lancashire historian John Marshall has recently written, 'In looking to the future, Burnley, like other towns of its kind, needs reminders of its past greatness. Just as urgently, it needs, for the benefit of future generations, a constant strengthening of a sense of its own identity. It is very important that the every-widening gaps between generations are closed rather than widened, so that Burnley children will have a chance to lean respect for the ways in which their forefathers earned their bread.' Dr Marshall concludes by asking whether the Burnley children of the future would learn about the Industrial Revolution from text-books. If the Weavers' Triangle can be saved, it can be a living text-book not only for Burnley people but for countless others from all over the world. (Powell, 1980: np)

SAVE's report recognised the importance of retaining historic fabric in strengthening connections both between generations and between children and place. Nurturing attachments is not just about ensuring the continuity of an individual's relationship with place but also that these relationships can be strengthened and adapted over generations. Memory is not just something in the past or a nostalgic reflection on the history of place but rather an active agent in nurturing intergenerational attachments to place. In these ways memory and emotion were recognised within campaigns and community engagement initiatives.

The ability to recognise memories and attachments was evident in the case of the redevelopment of the former Royal Infirmary, now named Quartermile, in Edinburgh, where built environment professionals attempted to understand who would be part of their engagement exercises and what mattered to these communities. This was tricky given the context of the complex which was a former hospital site that was relatively hidden within the everyday urban environment and people only spent time there out of necessity, whether as a medical worker, patient, or visitor. Establishing their communities to engage with and understanding who was likely to have an emotional relationship to the site was therefore a challenging task, made even harder given that the site started to be developed before social media provided a medium through which professionals could ascertain the responses and attachments of emotional communities. However, built environment professionals reflected on working with a range of different communities, from workers to patients, and how this could reveal attachments to the former hospital site. As a result of this engagement, built environment professionals were able to synthesise the information into a hierarchy of places which generated stronger and more widespread emotional attachments. The former Nurses Home – the Red Home (Figure 10) – and the Simpson's Memorial Maternity Pavilion (Figure 11) were each believed to be the locus of emotional attachments.

> There were emotional attachments to the Red Home. There were ... The Red Home I think a lot of people felt ... 'I was a nurse, and I spent years in that as a nurses' accommodation' so there was a little bit of that, there was a little bit of stuff ... but I don't think the community felt that ownership ... The only building there was a bigger attachment to was the Simpson's building which was the birthing unit, if you like, and there was a lot of attachment to that.   (Nathan)

Aaron built on this to state that there was an 'incredible emotional attachment' to the Maternity Pavilion, 'not because actually the quality of that fabric but because almost everyone in Edinburgh was born there and had their children born there. So you're really touching something that, it's a very raw nerve'. These attachments to parts of the former hospital complex that were expressed by a range of different people from staff, patients, and parents were not, however, strong enough to ensure that all the buildings remained. Thomas recalled that 'probably one of the most contentious aspects of the whole site masterplan related to the demolition of the chapel on the site' because people had gone through 'some very happy times but also some very sad times, where people had used that chapel facility, and had tremendous emotional attachment to it'.

Thomas went further to acknowledge that recognising these attachments took an emotional toll on all involved:

Figure 10 Red Home

Source: Canmore, Historic Environment Scotland: DP 028963 © Crown Copyright: HES. All Rights' Reserved.

Figure 11 Simpson's Memorial Maternity Pavilion

Source: Canmore, Historic Environment Scotland: SC 1174629 © Courtesy of HES (Scottish Colorfoto Collection). All Rights' Reserved.

> So yeah, the emotional attachment was quite a big issue for us and when it came to dealing with objections, people were in some cases being very, very open about, 'Cannot possibly demolish this chapel because I went through ... ' and you got the whole story. Sometimes it was a birth, sometimes it was a death, sometimes it was baby death ... it was just everything under the sun that you would associate with a massive hospital complex like it was. So yeah, it was quite a lot to deal with in all of that, and when you are living and breathing something like that, you get drawn into it. And you have to, I feel in a way you have to, to an extent anyway, to be able to understand the points that were being made and to give a fair response to it, and sometimes, I'm sure not all the objectors would have considered our responses possibly fair, but you tried your best.

Emotion, however, was not seen, as built environment professional Lorraine recognised, as a 'material consideration' within planning and therefore could not override the other factors on the site. What can and cannot be a material consideration is broad and subject to change. For example, Mark stated:

> Even the definition of material considerations, the legal definition says everything is capable of being a material consideration, which is of course no help to anyone who ever asks the question, what is or isn't material? Everything is capable of being as long as you ground it in planning policy.

However, in Lorraine's view, emotion, and the attachment that people had for the Red Home, Simpson's Maternity Pavilion, and the Chapel, could not be validated through the planning process for Quartermile. Emotions were therefore recognised by built environment professionals but there was no formal outlet for them within the existing heritage and planning system. In the case of Quartermile, emotion provided background information as part of community engagement exercises. This resulted in two different futures for the buildings that were the locus of emotional attachments. The Red Home, after much wrangling, was partly retained in an uneasy compromise and Simpson's Memorial Maternity Pavilion and Chapel were demolished. Existing attachments to place were therefore recognised as one variable within a complex array of competing factors that also included a focus on ensuring that new attachments to an award-winning new development could be created.

Negotiating New Emotional Relationships

Urban areas are not static, frozen in time and sheltered from change and neither are people's emotional relationships with places. Instead just as urban areas change so too do our relationships with them. We are therefore continually negotiating our emotional relationships with historic urban places. Within this context it is important to ask the extent to which different types of development help us to negotiate new emotional relationships.

A striking example of this was the extent to which 'human scale' was considered within new developments and in particular SAVE's focus on ensuring the aesthetic design of new places respected the ways in which people engaged in place. Indeed SAVE's focus on the emotional relationships that people have with their places as outlined in Section 4 translated into a desire to respect and nurture these relationships within urban design, architecture, and planning. Here, there was a call to actively validate the human-scale and to prioritise it within urban redevelopment initiatives across the United Kingdom:

> What is at stake is the human scale and the human face of London. Traditional terrace housing, plainfare though it may sometimes be, is almost never more than two or three windows wide. Thus for every three windows there is a door on the street and often a shop as well, ensuring that people are constantly walking in and out of buildings. By contrast the monolithic blocks that have replaced similar terraces nearby sometimes contain but a single entrance on each side, indeed in some cases a whole side of a block is without an entrance at all. This kills all life and variety at street level.   (Andreae, 1981: np)

Human-scale in this conceptualisation is not just the aesthetic preserve of urban designers, architects, and planners, but moreover is crucial to the everyday experiences that this Element has shown underpin the formation, disruption, and intensity of emotional attachments. A number of built environment professionals discussed the importance of designing for human-scale:

> It's the human scale, it's patina, it's traditional architecture, spaces that are made for people rather than cars usually. And those kind of spaces lend themselves to also activities, so you can have cafes and restaurants etc. there, outside spaces and that kind of thing. We all know what the good spaces are, you know why are there a million people in Covent Garden every day? 'cause it's obviously got such a great sense of place, you know 'cause it's got everything.   (Howard)

Attributing sense of place to historic urban areas was also discussed by built environment professionals. Cassie talked of the ways in which history is used as a 'starting point for an identity of a place' as well as 'to create new emotional attachments, and a new sense of place', while Lorraine used different language as she moved to discuss the 'feel' of a site in order to understand the existing and future emotional resonance of the historic place:

> I guess we're very much about place making, design and place making, and how do places work? If you look down somewhere does it feel that you want

to go into it? ... we did look at what are those views, what do the views feel like, how do people interact with the space, how do they move through it? So it is about that movement, emotional connection, how do people ... do people feel welcome, does the space too small that people won't feel welcome to go through it? So that does form part of the decision-making process.

The way historic places feel to local residents was a recurring issue. In Section 2, issues surrounding scaffolding were repeatedly brought up with residents expressing conventionally negative emotional responses. Understanding the way places make you feel is not new, as Worskett (1969) remarked, 'The townscape is of course, not just a matter of bricks and mortar; it is also concerned with atmosphere and personal experience. The architect on the planning team must get the feel of the townscape and communicate that experience to his colleagues' (119). However, gaining this insight into the feel of place was difficult as there were 'no standard methodologies' as 'It's not written down really anywhere or any methodology' (Lorraine). Despite this, a number of built environment professionals talked about spending their time trying to get the feel of different historic places and using this as a way to inform design decisions. Jean, for example, remembered 'having lots of conversation' about the Quartermile site 'to try and explain how it would feel within the site, because you're talking about big buildings ... so if you put a person in that, what are the proportions and how do those proportions reflect the proportions of other parts of Edinburgh? What kind of street will this feel like?' Callum went one further by stating:

> I find if you want to inspire a great creative ... then give them a big, emotional brief. So if I want to inspire a great masterplanner, I don't say, 'How many units can I get on that site?' and, 'How many office buildings can I get on that site?' I tell them a story. I ask them to show that piece of land so much respect, because what we're going to do is do something that lasts for 100 years.

In their different ways, built environment professionals tried to imagine the look and feel of the place through the built environment and through the stories that the built environment did and could narrate.

Built environment professionals also discussed the feel of historic places and related this to investment decisions. For example, Lesley discussed how businesses will co-locate near St Paul's Cathedral as 'people will go to the roof, people love showing ... they love having the headquarters there, "Look at St Paul's"'. Nathan further developed this aspect by outlining why people may make an investment decision to either live or work in or near historic buildings

> So I think when ... prestige and old stuff, gives people a sense of ... and especially nice old stuff ... old stuff, cleaned up old stuff, there's a prestige in

> that ... wanna live in it necessarily ... But I think most people are not like that. I think most people are like ... they want the association, but they don't necessarily want the upkeep, the maintenance; they're quite practical, people, at the end of the day, and that's probably why ... and the modern buildings here were more popular.

This was counterbalanced by Archie, who believed that emotional relationships with former industrial buildings could also inform a decision to live in a historic place:

> This was about the emotion of when you buy a loft, what does that enable me to do? That enables me to create my own destiny, to shape my own future. Again, it is where you are on that cycle. It is confidence. You are buying a shell, but you are buying it in a great location.

In these examples, there is a recognition that the juxtaposition of historic and modern produces emotional responses – pride and love – supported by investment decisions to locate either near, or in Archie's case, in a historic building. Built environment professionals recognise the multifarious ways in which people form emotional relationships with historic buildings and weigh this up alongside other factors including price, value, legislation, and location. Common across this is a recognition that historic places play a role in mobilising future attachments to place. The most explicit aspect of this mobilisation is seen during the process of place marketing. Stories embedded in historic urban places are often used to ensure that new investment, both human and capital, is predicated on building an emotional relationship between a potential investor and a redeveloped place. Here the role of emotion in 'selling places' is evident

> I think history probably does sell. Certainly in a world where what you are trying to do – or what I think we are trying to do; people might not express it in this way – certainly for retail where we are seriously, severely challenged by internet and all the rest of it, what you are trying to do is create an emotional response. (Grace)

> It's a massive selling point. Not everyone loves historic buildings, but a large proportion of the population do and if you buy one of our properties you can feel proud to be part of that whole story. (Phil)

The extent to which this was seen as successful was however debated by local residents. In Selkirk, this was based on a belief that 'you can't manufacture history and tradition. And we have it in Selkirk in spades, but as I said before, we just probably don't sell it enough' (Donnie). However, in Rothesay whether the 'right' characteristics were being 'sold' was brought up by Cameron, who contemplated the everydayness of place:

> one of the things that with all the historical stuff in Rothesay, just thinking whilst you were talking there, is that actually most of it is used on a day-to-day basis. So people will go into the Victorian toilets for a pee[13], so they use it as a toilet so it's not a, we must stand back and preserve this as being something that's . . . being heritage as used.

The fact that historic urban places could provoke emotional responses was seen as a selling point within the urban development process, yet the extent to which this reflected the authentic lived and felt experiences of place was questioned. In addition, the extent to which emotional attachments rather than responses are favoured in this process largely depends on the type of investment being made. For example, a place-based entrepreneur investing for the long-term and wanting to secure a reliable profit is more likely to be attuned to the need for a place to have the capacity for multiple and durable attachments to form and therefore be aware of the need to nurture everyday lived and felt experiences. On the other hand, a different type of developer may instead need to build and extract profit straight away in order to move to a different site and so be more interested in generating positive emotional responses that motivate people to invest in the short term and be less concerned with how these responses turn into attachments over time.

Conclusion

This section has demonstrated that historic urban places matter emotionally but that the reasons for why they matter are often hidden or neglected within existing processes within heritage and planning. Through using the tripartite conceptual framework set out in Table 1, it is possible to recognise where emotional responses, attachments, and communities can be located within policies and processes. Evidence from this section suggests that emotion is implicit in a number of macro-level policies in both the heritage and planning sectors and can be located within a number of place-based decision-making processes. Within this, there were a series of smaller and larger-scale interventions that included understanding how emotion helps to develop national and local campaigns, engage communities in formal consultation, inform urban design and architectural decisions both for buildings and areas, and influence place-marketing strategies. In these ways, we can engage with Sara Ahmed's question 'What do emotions do?'. In the context of this section, they can be seen to partially influence

---

[13] For more details, see the Category A listed West Pier Public Convenience: https://portal.historicenvironment.scot/designation/LB40448

decisions, meaning that while emotion can be recognised at different times within urban development, it is rarely a driver or fully validated within these systems.

6 Conclusion: A Future for Emotion

Historic urban places matter emotionally. This is demonstrated by the fact that historic urban places can provoke a range of emotional responses, stimulate emotional attachments, and produce emotional communities. These responses, attachments, and communities result from the psycho-emotional resonances of our everyday lived and felt experiences of place as much as from the architectural and historic interest of historic urban places. However, while it is important to note that not all places provoke responses or attachments and not all people form strong attachments, the overarching finding from this Element is that people can and do form emotional relationships with historic places. Within this context, the extent to which emotion can be recognised and validated within existing heritage and planning systems varies. Throughout this Element, the intention has been to unlock why historic places matter emotionally and to provide a conceptual framework that can help us make sense of the complex, profound, and rich reasons why. However, this conceptual framework need not stand in intellectual isolation, and it is my hope that the framework can also be seen as a methodological approach that can be adopted by researchers, communities, and built environment professionals to be able to unlock and convey why their historic places matter emotionally. In so doing, I recognise that the framework could evolve and be adapted to ensure that our emotional relationships to historic places are given more attention and can be further understood. As such, I conclude this Element by emphasising the four key aspects of the framework and using these aspects to consider possible futures for emotion and place.

First, each of the three components of the framework – responses, attachments, and communities – are vital and indeed are inextricably connected. We cannot consider attachments without responses, and we cannot consider either responses or attachments without considering the communities that hold emotional relationships with place. Over time, and dependent on context, other elements could also be added to this framework, but I would suggest that these three areas, each building on long-standing academic areas of research from across the arts, humanities, social, and natural sciences, provide a robust and rigorous starting point for exploring our emotional relationships with historic places.

Second, within the context of urban change, the Element argues that attachment is the key component. Attachment is deliberately located as the central element in the structure of the framework, demonstrating a belief that it is the glue that holds people and place together over time. The extent to which attachments to place are nurtured or disrupted during urban change affects not just the sense of place but also the sense of self. Within this context, emotional responses often provide a visible entry point into understanding that people may have attachments to place. However, a focus on emotional responses cannot tell us why historic urban places matter, either existentially for our ontological (in)security or experientially in terms of our daily lives, but they do give us a clue that these places matter so much to people that they can feel and express anger, joy, hope, sadness, excitement, fear, pride, and so on. Responses, whether isolated, blended, or mixed, are therefore one way, alongside studying actions and decisions, to surface the attachments of emotional communities.

If we return to the football stadium vignette from Section 1, we can easily identify the range of emotional responses that I and the emotional communities I belong to may express. On some match days this would be happiness, joy, and a sense of 'wow' and wonder from the sporting moments that take the breath away. On other match days, anger, disappointment, and sadness resulting from the final score, or even a neutrality or indifference may dominate. I may be joined in these responses by my fellow home fans – an audible emotional community that reveals every emotion as it courses through our individual and collective bodies and expressed through our cheers, jeers, and groans. We are not, however, the only emotional community: the away fans, the players, the club staff, and the referees each go through their own range of responses, which can often overlap and/or be in tension with ours. A focus on individual and collective responses thus might tell us how people feel in place in a particular moment in time. A scientific test may find a relatively high heart rate, sweaty palms, and high brain activity. If you were to ask me 'how do you feel' I may respond with 'annoyed', 'elated', 'gutted', or 'bored', and if I was asked to fill out a survey determining how satisfied I was with the place my answers would likely be conditioned by my emotional state. If you asked me in the seventh minute, I may be happy yet stressed, by the tenth minute I could be furious and sad, and by the ninetieth minute bored yet relieved.

However, while the specifics of my emotional responses can change, what is unlikely to change is the deeper sense of emotional attachment I feel for my stadium. I know that I feel a profound attachment to this historic urban place precisely because it actively shapes the stories of my life. This stadium allows me to create memories and to share heightened emotional experiences with friends and family and these feelings endure. They are woven into my mind and body, so much so that any potential threat to the physical fabric awakens in me a sense of attachment. It's my special place and my memories are nested within a shared and collective sense of place. In the context of ontological (in)security, I need to believe that I can continue to nurture my attachment over time. I guess I am saying that I need to have trust and hope that any discussion about the future for my stadium will both recognise and validate this attachment and involve me, or those like me – the hundreds of thousands of us who have invested their time, money, and – crucially – emotions in place over decades and through generations. Without this, a sense of fear, anger, sadness, and disappointment will dominate, as my attachment is at best disrupted and at worst severed. For urban change to be genuinely people-centred, I argue it needs to recognise and validate emotional attachments to place.

Third, I want to put forward the methodological approach that has resulted from the conceptual framework. In essence, this approach is the one I would follow if I wanted to understand why a place mattered emotionally.

Process

Figure 12 is not a flow chart and therefore does not impose a staged approach but rather outlines each of the elements needed to unlock why a place matters emotionally. A staged approach could, however, start with either identifying responses and using this to identify communities or mapping communities and using this to identify responses. Either way the process would not stop there but would instead be used to unravel what people are attached to and why.

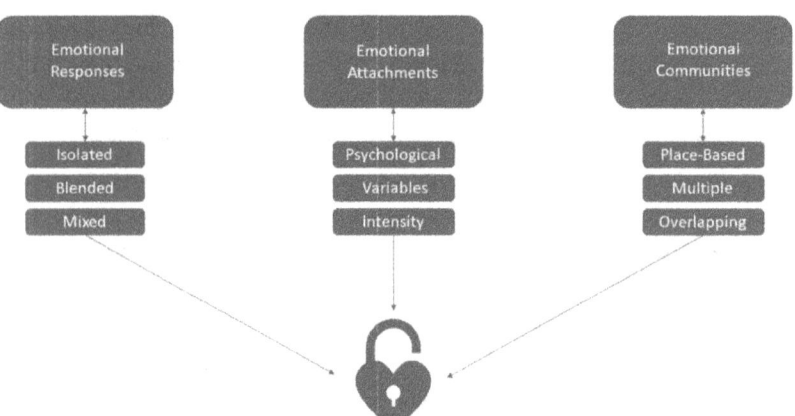

Figure 12 How to unlock why historic urban places matter emotionally
Source: R. Madgin. All Rights' Reserved.

Sources and Methods

As outlined in Section 1, choosing methods that foreground emotion, either through methods such as emoji workshops or through analysis techniques that prioritise emotion words, themes, and actions, is crucial to revealing the emotional relationships between people and place. Valid data can therefore be created by using emotion-based methods, which is a growing area within heritage theory and practice. For example, a number of methodologies that foreground heritage and emotion were explored and evaluated by researchers and practitioners across Africa, Asia, Europe, North America, Oceania, and South America including neuroscientific, observational, survey and digital to reveal that sources and methods can reveal emotional attachments to historic places (Madgin and Lesh, 2021). Crucial within this process is that there can be variety in how emotional information is expressed, collected, and received (Madgin and Robson, 2023), that Arnstein's ladder can be remixed to ensure that 'innovative practices' are 'rooted in local knowledge' (Roberts and Kelly, 2019: 301), and that new, more inclusive (Crichton-Turley, 2023), and emotionally informed practices can be built from adopting these innovative approaches to sources and methods.

Analysis

Within this, I suggest examining responses both in isolation and together. Isolation tells us why people feel proud, for example of Paisley Abbey, and therefore helps us to understand place but, by itself, is somewhat reductionist and simplifies our emotional relationships with places. We know from the evidence in this Element that responses are plural and fluid and that, for example, Campbeltown Town Hall provokes pride and happiness, and scaffolding stimulates a complex array of positive and negative responses. From there, it is possible to explore the ways in which these individual responses are shared by others and are related to existential and everyday concerns. The conclusion of this exercise should result in an understanding of the intensity of attachment held by different emotional communities and the reasons why these feelings exist. A final stage could then be to use this information as part of place-based decision-making and some possible options to achieve this are discussed later in this section.

The fourth and final key aspect of this framework is that it moves us away from binary distinctions between emotion and objectivity in the context of decision-making. This belief in the existence of such a binary has long remained core to professional practice in the Western world and is deeply rooted in philosophical positions (Jones and Yarrow, 2022). However, over the course of doing this research and writing this Element, rhetoric about 'emotion', 'heritage', and 'place' in the context of placemaking has developed so quickly that it feels like we have now reached a crossroads. We have acknowledgements from professional organisations that 'heritage fosters a strong sense of belonging and attachment to place' (Historic England, 2020: 18), place is 'emotional as well as practical' (Grayston and Lloyd, 2023: 9), 'people experience place emotionally' (Quality of Life Foundation, 2022: 5) emotion is a central part of the function of design (Heatherwick, 2023), and 'pride in place', belonging and attachment became a key part of the political landscape (HM Government, 2022). At a local level, there is a belief that 'people-centred attachment to place, therefore, as a complement to conservation or regeneration of material fabric of the city becomes of significant importance in pursuit of planning, regeneration . . . and of placemaking' (Evans, 2022). Thus, now more than ever, it feels like the collective mindset is shifting to recognise the importance of emotion within heritage and placemaking. However, much of this still rests with rhetoric and it is still doubtful if emotion can yet be recognised as a valid category of information by existing systems. At this point in the crossroads, we need to consider the extent to which our evolving rhetoric is matched by systems that can move away from seeing 'emotions as a source of bias and distortion' (Hoch, 2006: 367) and towards seeing emotion as a valid category of information that can further inform people-centred decision-making in the urban environment. My hope is that by providing a conceptual framework and outlining its potential application (Figure 12) it becomes possible to see how this can be achieved. As the evidence in this Element demonstrates, emotion, in the form of responses, attachments, and communities, can be a category of information that can help inform the type, nature, and extent of urban change.

So what could a future for emotion and place look like? In an academic context, debates still rage as to how many emotional responses exist, how emotions are accessed, how we develop attachments, and the messiness of emotional communities. Therefore there is still much to build on in the realm of emotion. Within critical heritage studies much remains in terms of understanding how emotion informs values, significance, working practices, as well as the contestation and reception of historic places. In particular, we have much to learn around the emotional dimensions of contested spaces, the marginalisation of certain emotions, communities, and places, why and how we do not form attachments to some historic places, and how emotional regimes condition the production and reception of public emotions in historic places, to name just four areas.

In the context of professional practice, we could, at one extreme, accept that 'emotion', in the form of responses, attachments, and communities, matters and do no more with it. In the context of heritage designation we could go to the other end of the spectrum and create a further category of emotional value to sit within the existing *Conservation Principles* (England) or the *Principles for Selection and Designation* (Scotland). In the context of heritage management, we could suggest that emotional attachment be a material consideration within heritage and planning policies and practices, or we could build it into urban design practices. These are potentially seismic actions that therefore need deliberative, sustained, and collective consideration from a range of people including local residents, built environment professionals, and academics recognising that opening the door on emotion, in the form of responses, attachments, and communities could have real consequences for the systems that guide change as well as the emotional relationships that exist between people and place.

If we accept that emotion, in the form of responses, attachments, and communities, is key to the evolution of people-centred approaches to place-making then different decisions may be possible within the remit of existing policies and practices. These could be relatively small-scale 'quick wins', such as ensuring that people's attachment to the clock on the clock tower in Selkirk was validated by ensuring it was visible throughout the conservation works. Or it could be on a larger scale. For example, community engagement exercises could use emotionally informed methods to surface emotional attachments; the use of a particular historic place could be considered in the context of attachment; and/or inexpensive access to restored buildings could be prioritised within ongoing discussions about future uses. We could hear and validate the attachments expressed through the emotional language used in planning objections, committees, and public inquiries. Attachments could also be woven through policy documentation and guidance so that they were explicit rather than implicit and became obvious rather than hidden and only revealed during change. Forewords to masterplans could be 'crowd written', or otherwise expressed through film, animation, mapping, and/or podcasts, by place-based emotional communities; local place/neighbourhood plans could include a section on people's attachments to historic places; and conservation area appraisals and listed building descriptions could consider emotion, in the form of responses, attachments, and communities, over time and show how this has ebbed and flowed. Each of these initiatives would provide explicit information as to what is meaningful to a range of emotional communities and thus why historic places matter emotionally. In these ways we can start with the multiple meanings embedded in historic urban places and use them to nurture and build attachments as places undergo change.

If this process was accepted, then different outcomes may be possible. For example, underpinning this framework is a belief that developing a better understanding of why historic places matter emotionally can lead to better socio-economic outcomes for people and place (Madgin and Howcroft, 2024). This belief is supported by a growing evidence base that focuses on the positive connections between (1) emotion and economic development (Gallup, 2010) and (2) health and well-being (National Trust, 2019; Soafer and Gallou, 2022). This body of work promises much in terms of demonstrating the positive consequences of having an emotional relationship with place, whether that is at a neighbourhood level, or a heritage site owned by the National Trust and/or English Heritage. The conceptual framework outlined in this Element provides an understanding of how people form emotional relationships with historic urban places and this is as an essential first step towards being able to further evidence the impacts of these relationships for people and place.

This Element has outlined why historic urban places matter emotionally and showed the ways in and extent to which emotion shapes decision-making in the urban environment. The Element demonstrates that our emotional relationships with places do not have to remain neglected and hidden only to be unlocked through a crisis moment and they do not have to remain implicit within the process of urban change. Instead, we can take heart from the evidence within this Element to recognise the rich reasons why historic places matter emotionally and use this to work towards validating emotion within future theories and practices. My hope in writing this Element is that this conceptual framework, which sees emotion as comprised of responses, attachments, and communities, can be used as a way to support further inquiry into how we can work inclusively, productively, and genuinely with emotion in ways that can both enrich and nourish our sense of self and place.

References

Ahmed, S. A. (2014). *The Cultural Politics of Emotion*, 2nd ed. Edinburgh: Edinburgh University Press.

Altman, I., and Low, S. M. (eds.). (1992). *Place Attachment*. Boston: Springer US.

Archer, A., and Wildman, N. (eds.) (2021). *Emotions in Sport and Games*. London: Taylor and Francis Group.

Ashworth, G. J. (1997). Conservation as Preservation or as Heritage: Two Paradigms and Two Answers. *Built Environment*, 23(2), 92–102.

Bandarin, F., and Oers, R. van. (2012). *The Historic Urban Landscape: Managing Heritage in an Urban Century*. Hoboken: John Wiley & Sons.

Baum, H. (2015). Planning with Half a Mind: Why Planners Resist Emotion. *Planning Theory & Practice*, 16(4), 498–516.

Berrios, R., Totterdell, P., and Kellett, S. (2015). Eliciting Mixed Emotions: A Meta-analysis Comparing Models, Types, and Measures. *Frontiers in Psychology*, 6, article 428.

Borén, T., Grzyś, P., and Young, C. (2021). Policy-Making as an Emotionally Charged Arena: The Emotional Geographies of Urban Cultural Policy-Making. *International Journal of Cultural Policy*, 27(4), 449–62.

Byrne, D., and Nugent. M. (2004). *Mapping Attachment: A Spatial Approach to Aboriginal Post-contact Heritage*. Sydney: Department of Environment and Conservation.

CHCfE Consortium (2015). *Cultural Heritage Counts for Europe*. Krakow: CHCfE Consortium.

Council of Europe (2005). *Framework Convention on the Value of Cultural Heritage for Society*. Strasbourg: Council of Europe.

Craggs, R., Geoghegan, H., and Neate. H. (2016). Managing Enthusiasm: Between 'Extremist' Volunteers and 'Rational' Professional Practices in Architectural Conservation. *Geoforum*, 74, 1–8.

Cresswell, T. (2014). *Place: An Introduction*, 2nd ed. Oxford: Wiley-Blackwell.

Crichton-Turley, C. E. (2023). Researching Heritage and History with Underserved Communities. Sheffield: University of Sheffield. https://sites.google.com/sheffield.ac.uk/roots-and-futures/toolkit.

Crossick, G., and Kaszynska, P. (2016). *Understanding the Value of Arts and Culture*. Swindon: UKRI.

de Bakker, M. (2022). Between Place and Territory: Young People's Emotional Geographies of Security and Insecurity in Brussels' Deprived Areas. *Emotion, Space and Society*, 45, article 100911.

Department for Communities and Local Government (2011). *Assets of Community Value – Policy Statement.* London: Department for Communities and Local Government.

Department of Levelling Up, Housing and Communities (2023). *National Planning Policy Framework.* London: Department of Levelling Up, Housing and Communities.

Desmet, P. M. A., Porcelijn, R., and Van Dijk, M. B. (2007). Emotional Design: Application of a Research-Based Design Approach. *Knowledge, Technology & Policy*, 20(3), 141–55.

Edwards, S., and Purohit, R. (2023). *CCQOL Inclusive Engagement Toolkit Final.* https://www.qolf.org/wp-content/uploads/Inclusive_Engagement_Tookit_Final.pdf.pdf.

Ekman, P. (1992). An Argument for Basic Emotions. *Cognition and Emotion*, 6 (3/4), 169–200.

English Heritage (2008). *Conservation Principles, Policies and Guidance.* Swindon: English Heritage.

Evans, B. (ed.) (2022). *People Make Places because Glasgow Belongs to You: Report of the Place Commission, Glasgow.* Glasgow: Glasgow Urban Laboratory.

Fallon, E. (2022). How Property Developers Make Decisions: Dublin 2010–2020. Unpublished PhD thesis. Glasgow: University of Glasgow.

Feldman Barrett, L. (2017). *How Emotions are Made: The Secret Life of the Brain.* London: Macmillan.

Ferreira, A. (2013). Emotions in Planning Practice: A Critical Review and a Suggestion for Future Developments based on Mindfulness. *The Town Planning Review*, 84(6), 703–19.

Frevert, U., Bailey, C., Eitler, P., Gammerl, B., Hitzer, B., Pernau, M., Scheer, M., Schmidt, A., and Verheyen, N. (eds.) (2014). *Emotional Lexicons: Continuity and Change in the Vocabulary of Feeling 1700–2000*, 1st ed. Oxford: Oxford University Press.

Fried, M. (2000). Continuities and Discontinuities of Place. *Journal of Environmental Psychology*, 20(3), 193–205.

Fullilove, M. T. (2016). *Root Shock: How Tearing Up City Neighborhoods Hurts America, And What We Can Do About It.* New York: New York University Press.

Gallup (2011). *Soul of the Community.* Knight Foundation. https://knightfoundation.org/sotc/.

Giddens, A. (1990). *The Consequences of Modernity.* Cambridge: Polity Press.

Gieryn, T. F. (2000). A Space for Place in Sociology. *Annual Review of Sociology*, 26, 463–96.

Graham, H., Mason, R., and Newman, A. (2009). Literature Review: Historic Environment, Sense of Place and Social Capital. https://historicengland.org.uk/content/heritage-counts/pub/sense_of_place_lit_review_web1-pdf/.

Grayston, R., and Lloyd, T. (2023). *The Case for Place: Creating Prosperity through the Economics of Attraction*. A Report by Create Streets Foundation for Karbon Home. London: Create Streets.

Great Britain (1969). *People and Planning: Report of the Committee on Public Participation in Planning*. London: HMSO.

Gregory, J. (2015). Connecting with the Past through Social Media: The 'Beautiful Buildings and Cool Places Perth has Lost' Facebook Group. *International Journal of Heritage Studies*, 21(1), 22–45.

Grenville, J. (2007). Conservation as Psychology: Ontological Security and the Built Environment. *International Journal of Heritage Studies*, 13(6), 447–61.

  (2015). Ontological Security in a Post-Crash World – A Tale of Two Yorkshire Cities. *Heritage & Society*, 8(1), 43–59.

Grosvenor (2019). *Rebuilding Trust*. Discussion Paper. London: Grosvenor.

Grosvenor (2020). *Creating a More Positive Space: Our Community Charter*. London: Grosvenor.

Harrison, R. (2004). *Shared Landscapes: Archaeologies of Attachment and the Pastoral Industry in New South Wales*. Sydney: University of New South Wales Press.

Heatherwick, T. (2023). *Humanise: A Maker's Guide to Building Our World*. New York: Viking.

Historic England (2017). *Conservation Principles for the Sustainable Management of the Historic Environment: Consultation Draft*. London: Historic England. http://cms.historicengland.org.uk/content/docs/guidance/conservation-principles-consultation-draft-pdf.

  (2020). *Heritage Counts: Heritage and Society*. London: Historic England.

Historic Environment Scotland (2017). *What's Your Heritage, Past, Places and Traditions*. Edinburgh: Historic Environment Scotland.

  (2019). *Designation Policy and Selection Guidance*. Edinburgh: Historic Environment Scotland.

Historic Scotland (2009). *Scottish Historic Environment Policy*. Edinburgh: Historic Scotland.

Historic Scotland (2011). *Scottish Historic Environment Policy*. Edinburgh: Historic Scotland.

HM Government (2022). *The White Paper: Levelling up the United Kingdom*. London: HM Government.

HM Government (2024). *Update on the Pride in Place Mission:* https://assets.publishing.service.gov.uk/media/65b2348bf2718c0014fb1d29/Narrative_for_Pride_in_Place.pdf.

Hoch, C. (2006). Emotions and Planning. *Planning Theory & Practice*, 7(4), 367–82.

House of Commons Debate (14 April 1875), vol. 223 cc881.

House of Commons Debate (14 April 1875), vol. 223 cc905.

Hubbard, P. (1993). The Value of Conservation: A Critical Review of Behavioural Research. *Town Planning Review*, 64, 359–73.

ICOMOS. (1994). *The Nara Document on Authenticity*. Paris: ICOMOS.

(1996). *The Declaration of San Antonio*. Paris: ICOMOS.

(2008). *Québec Declaration on the Preservation of the Spirit of Place*. Paris: ICOMOS.

ICOMOS Australia (2013) [1999] [1979]. *Charter for the Conservation of Places of Cultural Significance* (The Burra Charter), revised 1999 and 2013. Melbourne: ICOMOS.

Inch A., Sartorio F., Bishop J., Beebeejaun Y., McClymont K., Frediani AA., Cociña C, and Quick, K. S. (2019). *Planning Theory & Practice*, special issue, *People and Planning at Fifty*, 20(5), 735–59.

Israelsson, A., Seiger, A., and Laukka, P. (2023). Blended Emotions Can Be Accurately Recognized from Dynamic Facial and Vocal Expressions. *Journal of Nonverbal Behaviour*, 47, 267–84.

Jivén, G., and Larkham, P. J. (2003). Sense of Place, Authenticity and Character: A Commentary. *Journal of Urban Design*, 8(1), 67–81.

Johnston, C. (1992). *What Is Social Value?* Canberra: Australian Government and Publishing Service.

Jones, S. (2017). Wrestling with the Social Value of Heritage: Problems, Dilemmas and Opportunities. *Journal of Community Archaeology & Heritage*, 4(1), 21–37.

Jones, S., and Yarrow, T. (2022). *The Object of Conservation: An Ethnography of Conservation Practice*. London: Routledge.

Lecompte, A. F., Trelohan, M., Gentric, M., and Aquilina, M. (2017). Putting Sense of Place at the Centre of Place Brand Development. *Journal of Marketing Management*, 33(5–6), 400–20.

Lewicka, M. (2011). Place Attachment: How Far Have We Come in the Last 40 Years? *Journal of Environmental Psychology*, 31(3), 207–30.

Lowenthal, D. (2013). *The Past Is a Foreign Country – Revisited*. Cambridge: Cambridge University Press.

Lowenthal, D., & Binney, M. (eds.) (1981). *Our Past Before Us: Why Do We Save It?* London: T. Smith.

Lynch, K. (1960). *The Image of the City*. Massachusetts: MIT Press.
Madgin, R. (2019). A Place for Urban Conservation? The Changing Values of Glasgow's Built Heritage. In K. Kintrea and R. Madgin (eds.), *Transforming Glasgow beyond the Post-Industrial City*. Bristol: Policy Press, 221–38.

(2021a). *Why Do Historic Places Matter: Emotional Attachments to Urban Heritage*. Glasgow: University of Glasgow.

(2021b). *Personalities of Historic Urban Places*. Animation produced with We Are Cognitive. www.youtube.com/watch?v=ZshZ3Fv1O90.

(2021c). *How and Where do Emotional Attachments Influence Decision Making within the Urban Environment?* Infographic produced with We Are Cognitive. https://www.gla.ac.uk/schools/socialpolitical/research/research-projects/why-do-historic-places-matter/.

(2021d). Recognising Emotions in Urban Development. In K. Barclay and J. Riddle (eds.), *Urban Emotions and the Making of the City: Interdisciplinary Perspectives*. London: Routledge, 143–163

(2021e) Emoji as Method. In R. Madgin and J. Lesh (eds.), *People-Centred Methodologies for Heritage Conservation: Exploring Emotional Attachments to Historic Urban Places*. London: Routledge, 80–94

Madgin, R., and Howcroft, M. (2024). Advancing People-Centred, Place-Based Approaches, AHRC Place Programme Report, University of Glasgow, https://eprints.gla.ac.uk/342111/1/342111.pdf.

Madgin, R., and Lesh, J. (eds.) (2021). *People-Centred Methodologies for Heritage Conservation: Exploring Emotional Attachments to Historic Urban Places*. London: Routledge.

Madgin, R., and Robson, E. (2023). *Developing a People-Centred, Place-Led Approach: The Value of the Arts and Humanities*. Glasgow: University of Glasgow. https://www.gla.ac.uk/media/Media_978141_smxx.pdf.

Madgin, R., Bradley, L., and Hastings, A. (2016). Connecting Physical and Social Dimensions of Place Attachment: What Can We Learn from Attachment to Urban Recreational Spaces? *Journal of Housing and the Built Environment*, 31(4), 677–93.

Madgin, R., Webb, D., Ruiz, P., and Snelson, T. (2018). Resisting Relocation and Reconceptualising Authenticity: The Experiential and Emotional Values of the Southbank Undercroft, London, UK. *International Journal of Heritage Studies*, 24(6), 585–98.

Manzo, L. C. (2014). Exploring the Shadow Side: Place Attachment in the Context of Stigma, Displacement and Social Housing. In L. C. Manzo and P. Devine-Wright (eds.), *Place Attachment: Advances in Theory, Methods and Applications*. London: Routledge, 178–90.

Manzo, L. C., and Devine-Wright, P. (2021). *Place Attachment: Advances in Theory, Methods and Applications*. Abingdon: Routledge.

Marsh, N., Howcroft, M. and Owen, J. (2023). *Understanding Pride in Place. A Place-Based Creative Think Kit from Feeling Towns*. Southampton: University of Southampton.

Mayes, T. (2018). *Why Old Places Matter: How Historic Places affect our Identity and Well-Being*. Lanham: Rowman & Littlefield Publishers.

Mesquita, B. (2022). *Between Us: How Cultures Create Emotions*, 1st ed. New York: W.W. Norton & Company.

Miller, M. (2003). *The Representation of Place: Urban Planning and Protest in France and Great Britain, 1950-1980*. Aldershot: Ashgate.

National Trust (2017). *Places That Make Us*. Swindon: National Trust.

(2019). *Why Places Matters to People. Research Report*. Swindon: National Trust.

Page, M. (2016). *Why Preservation Matters*. New Haven: Yale University Press.

Pernau, M. (2017). Feeling Communities: Introduction. *The Indian Economic & Social History Review*, 54(1), 1–20.

Quality of Life Foundation and Landsec (2022). *Measuring Success: A Social Value Roundtable*. https://www.qolf.org/what-we-do/measuring-success-a-social-value-roundtable/.

Relph, E. (2008). *Place and Placelessness*. London: Pion.

Roberts, A., and Kelly, G. (2019). Remixing as Praxis: Arnstein's Ladder through the Grassroots Preservationist's Lens. *Journal of the American Planning Association*, 85(3), 301–20.

Rosenwein, B. H. (2006). *Emotional Communities in the Early Middle Ages*. New York: Cornell University Press.

Ruiz, P., Snelson, T., Madgin, R., and Webb, D. (2019). 'Look at What We Made': Communicating Subcultural Value on London's Southbank. *Cultural Studies*, 34(3), 392–417.

Scheer, M. (2012). Are Emotions a Kind of Practice (and Is That What Makes Them Have a History)? A Bourdieuian Approach to Understanding Emotion. *History and Theory*, 51(2), 193–220.

Schofield, J., and Szymanski, R. (eds.) (2010). *Local Heritage, Global Context: Cultural Perspectives on Sense of Place*. Farnham: Ashgate.

Scottish Government (2014). *Our Place in Time: The Historic Environment Strategy for Scotland*. Edinburgh: Scottish Government.

Scottish Government (2015). *Community Empowerment (Scotland) Act*. www.legislation.gov.uk/asp/2015/6/contents/enacted.

Smith, L. (2006). *Uses of Heritage*. London: Routledge.

(2020). *Emotional Heritage: Visitor Engagement at Museums and Heritage Sites*, 1st ed. Abingdon: Routledge.

Smith, L., and Campbell. G. (2015). The Elephant in the Room: Heritage, Affect, and Emotion. In W. Logan, M. Nic Craith, and U. Kockel (eds.), *A Companion to Heritage Studies*. Chichester: Wiley and Sons.

Smith, L., Wetherell, M., and Campbell, G. (eds.) (2018). *Emotion, Affective Practices, and the Past in the Present*. London: Routledge.

Smith, P. F. (1975), Conservation Myths (1): Facadism Used to be a Dirty Word. *Built Environment Quarterly*, 1(1), 77–80.

Soafer, J., and Gallou, E. (2022), Places of Joy: The Role of Heritage During the COVID-19 Pandemic. London: Historic England. https://historicengland.org.uk/whats-new/research/back-issues/places-of-joy-the-role-of-heritage-during-the-covid-19-pandemic/.

Stedman, R. (2003). Is It Really Just a Social Construction?: The Contribution of the Physical Environment to Sense of Place. *Society & Natural Resources*, 16(8), 671–85.

Swedish National Heritage Board. (2014). *Report from the Swedish National Heritage Board: The Faro Convention, Council of Europe Framework Convention on the Social Value of Cultural Heritage*. Stockholm: National Heritage Board

Tolia-Kelly, D. P., Waterton, E., and Watson, S. (2017). *Heritage, Affect and Emotion: Politics, Practices and Infrastructures*. London: Routledge.

Tracy, J. L., and Randles, D. (2011). Four Models of Basic Emotions: A Review of Ekman and Cordaro, Izard, Levenson, and Panksepp and Watt. *Emotion Review*, 3(4), 397–405.

Trower, S. (ed.) (2011). *Place, Writing, and Voice in Oral History*. New York: Palgrave Macmillan

Tuan, Y.-F. (1977). *Space and Place: The Perspective of Experience*. Minneapolis: University of Minnesota Press.

(1979). Space and Place: Humanistic Perspective. In S. Gale and G. Olsson (eds.), *Philosophy in Geography*. Dordrecht: Springer Netherlands, 387–427.

Wang, Y. (2023). Exploring Multiple Dimensions of Attachment to Historic Urban Places, a Case Study of Edinburgh, Scotland. *International Journal of Heritage Studies*, 29(5), 428–40.

Waterton, E., Smith, L., and Campbell, G. (2006). The Utility of Discourse Analysis to Heritage Studies: The Burra Charter and Social Inclusion. *International Journal of Heritage Studies*, 12(4), 339–55.

Wells, J. (2020). The Affect of Old Places. Exploring the Dimensions of Place Attachment and Senescent Environments. In D. Kopec and A. Bliss (eds.),

Place Meaning and Attachment: Authenticity, Heritage and Preservation. New York: Routledge, 1–15.

Wilkinson, A., (2006). SAVE Britain's Heritage and the Amenity Societies. *Journal of Architectural Conservation*, 12(3), 107–26.

Worskett, R. (1969). *The Character of Towns.* London: Architectural Association.

Zink, V. (2019). Affective Communities. In J. Slaby and C. von Scheve, *Affective Societies: Key Concepts.* London: Routledge, 289–99.

SAVE Britain's Heritage Reports

Andreae S. (1981). *London, One Damned Georgian Building, A Continuous Tragedy Currently Featuring the Comyn Ching Triangle.* London: SAVE Britain's Heritage.

Binney, M. (1979). *Satanic Mills: Industrial Architecture in the Pennines.* London: SAVE Britain's Heritage.

(1981). *The Colossus of Battersea: A Report.* London: SAVE Britain's Heritage.

(2005). *SAVE Britain's Heritage, 1975-2005. Thirty Years of Campaigning*, London: Scala.

(2016). *Big Saves. Heroic Transformations of Great Landmarks.* London: SAVE Britain's Heritage.

Binney, M. and Milne, E. (eds.) (1983). *Time Gentlemen Please!*, London: SAVE Britain's Heritage.

Binney, M. and Watson-Smyth, M. (1991). *SAVE Britain's Heritage Action Guide.* London: Collins & Brown.

Powell, K. (1980). *Burnley: Mill-Town Image Burden or Asset?* London: SAVE Britain's Heritage.

(1982a). *City Centre Carve Up.* London: SAVE Britain's Heritage.

(1982b). *Manchester: The Disappearing Cathedral Conservation Area.* London: Save Britain's Heritage and Victorian Society, Manchester Group.

(1982c). *What! Conservation in Gateshead?* London: SAVE Britain's Heritage

(1983). *Halifax: Historic Buildings at Risk.* London: SAVE Britain's Heritage.

(1986). *Leeds – A Lost Opportunity.* London: SAVE Britain's Heritage.

SAVE Britain's Heritage (1975). Why Save? *The Architect's Journal*, 17/24, 1288–89.

Wood, O. L., Freeman, J., and Binney, M. (1983). *From Splendour to Banality: The Rebuilding of the City of London, 1945–1983.* London: SAVE Britain's Heritage.

Acknowledgements

Understanding why historic places matter emotionally has been the focus of my work for a number of years. A number of people and organisations have worked with me, supported me, offered advice, and given me confidence that this was a worthwhile pursuit. I'd like to thank all those associated with the Arts and Humanities Research Council for funding this research and for consistently supporting work on heritage and place. I'm indebted to my project partners, Historic Environment Scotland, Montagu Evans LLP, and SAVE Britain's Heritage for their support and inspiration. In particular I want to thank Barbara Cummins, Elly McCrone, Chris Miele, Henrietta Billings, and Mike Fox, who provided leadership and guidance. In addition I'd like to thank the many other members of each organisation for shaping the methods, visiting historic urban places with me, discussing the findings, introducing me to your workplaces, producing the images, providing encouragement and support and much more. Your engagement with, and support of, the project means more to me than I can convey in words.

Thanks also to Tosh Warwick for initial input at a very early stage of the work as well as the members of the Project Advisory Board who provided moral support and practical advice throughout: Nigel Barker-Mills, Karen Brookfield, Danny Callaghan, Euan Leitch, Kevin Murray, and Fiona Newton. At the University of Glasgow I'd particularly like to thank Annette Hastings for her support, not just with this project, but over a long period of time. Crucially, I extend a huge thank you to all those involved with the research across England and Scotland – thank you so much for being so generous with your time, thoughts, and feelings about your places.

Thanks also to the University of Glasgow's Photographic Unit for help with images as well as the University of Glasgow's Knowledge Exchange Fund, Lucy Janes, and all those at We Are Cognitive for the animation and infographic found in this book.

Thanks to all those at Cambridge University Press who have made the publication process appear seamless. I'm particularly pleased to publish this Element with Cambridge University Press as they have consistently supported work in both urban history and heritage.

Getting to the stage where this Element became possible can only occur because of work that has gone before. As such I'd like to thank all those whose work is cited in the Element and all those who engaged with the work and gave feedback at conferences, seminars, and in the classroom. Ideas are built over time and the ones in this book are inspired by the collective endeavour of an academic, student, and practice community who commit every day to trying to move ideas forward in ways that can secure better outcomes for people in place. I am fortunate to work with some brilliant colleagues at the University of Glasgow. I am consistently inspired both by the content of your work and the considerate and collegial ways in which you work. Together this makes the Division of Urban Studies and Social Policy at the University of Glasgow a nurturing and supportive environment in which to teach, think, and act, and this Element is very much a product of this environment.

As ever, all views and any errors contained in this book are the responsibility of the author. The views expressed should not be assumed to be those of the University of Glasgow, the project partners, or the members of the project advisory board.

Funding from the Arts and Humanities Research Council (Grant Reference: AH/P007058/1) made it possible for this Element to be published open access, making the text in the digital version freely available for anyone to read and reuse under a Creative Commons licence. The images remain all rights reserved and held by the copyright owners marked in the captions. These are not part of the Creative Commons license and cannot be reused without prior written and express permission of the respective copyright holders.

This Element is dedicated to the memory of Barbara Cummins who sadly passed away in September 2024. Barbara was a supportive mentor, inspirational town planner and heritage specialist, and brilliant company.

Cambridge Elements ≡

Critical Heritage Studies

Kristian Kristiansen
University of Gothenburg

Michael Rowlands
UCL

About the Series

This series focuses on the recently established field of Critical Heritage Studies. Interdisciplinary in character, it brings together contributions from experts working in a range of fields, including cultural management, anthropology, archaeology, politics, and law. The series will include volumes that demonstrate the impact of contemporary theoretical discourses on heritage found throughout the world, raising awareness of the acute relevance of critically analysing and understanding the way heritage is used today to form new futures.

Cambridge Elements

Critical Heritage Studies

Elements in the Series

Understanding Islam at European Museums
Magnus Berg and Klas Grinell

Ethnographic Returns: Memory Processes and Archive Film
Anne Gustavsson

Global Heritage, Religion, and Secularism
Trinidad Rico

Heritage Making and Migrant Subjects in the Deindustrialising Region of the Latrobe Valley
Alexandra Dellios

Heritage and Design: Ten Portraits from Goa (India)
Pamila Gupta

Heritage, Education and Social Justice
Veysel Apaydin

Geopolitics of Digital Heritage
Natalia Grincheva and Elizabeth Stainforth

Here and Now at Historic Sites: Pupils and Guides Experiencing Heritage
David Ludvigsson, Martin Stolare and Cecilia Trenter

Heritage and Transformation of an African Popular Music
Aghi Bahi

Will Heritage Save Us? Intangible Cultural Heritage and the Sustainable Development Turn
Chiara Bortolotto

The Neoliberalisation of Heritage in Africa
Rachel King

Why Historic Places Matter Emotionally: Responses – Attachments – Communities
Rebecca Madgin

A full series listing is available at: www.cambridge.org/CHSE